Teacher Guide to Spelling and Word Meaning

Authors

Diane E. Paynter

Robert J. Marzano

John S. Kendall

Lorraine Marzano

Consultants

John Barell

Gladys Hillman-Jones

Zaner-Bloser

ISBN 0-88085-143-0

Zaner-Bloser, Inc., P.O. Box 16764, Columbus, Ohio 43216-6764

Printed in the United States of America

Although spelling has always been considered an important part of the language arts curriculum, recently it has been the focus of extensive research and theory development. The results of the research are very exciting and quite profound in their implications for instruction. First and foremost, the research and theory indicate that spelling development should be considered part of a much larger system of literacy development.

Second, the larger system of literacy development should be **literature based**. That is, students should develop the skills of literacy by reading good literature, writing about good literature, discussing it, reacting to it, and so on. However, this book is not designed to describe what a literature-based classroom should be like. For such a discussion, you should consult the *Literacy Plus Teacher Guide*. This book is designed to describe how spelling can be taught in a literature-based environment. A basic assumption underlying this approach to spelling instruction, then, is that the classroom is a literacy-rich environment and students within the classroom are continually involved in such activities as:

- selecting pieces of literature and reading them at their own pace.
- reacting to literature and discussing their reactions with the teacher and with peers.
- selecting topics about which to write and developing these topics.
- selecting words of interest from their reading and incorporating them into their vocabularies.
- thinking and reasoning critically and creatively about literacy and their own literacy development.

In addition to these assumptions, there are five principles that were used to guide the development of this approach to spelling. They are:
1. Spelling is a developmental process.
2. Formal spelling instruction should not occur until students are developmentally ready.
3. Writing should be the primary vehicle for building spelling skills.
4. Spelling should be taught in relation to word meaning.
5. Spelling instruction should involve student choice.

These principles are elaborated below.

Principle #1
Spelling Is a Developmental Process

In the past, educators have viewed spelling competence as an either-or proposition—either you could spell a word correctly or you couldn't. However, we know now that like any competency spelling ability develops over time and, in fact, progresses through predictable stages. Most teachers have become familiar with this concept under the general rubric of **invented spelling**.

Invented spelling refers to young children's initial best guess attempts to spell words. To illustrate, Figures 1a, b, and c show an example of a student's invented spelling and two samples of later developmental stages.

Figure 1a

Dear
leprechanr
Ges me a l
uor GoD
mI a bes is
2225 SOM EOL hort

Figure 1b

March 6.   Wensday
I   had   Chikin   fride.
State   at   school
and   my   mom   leFt
some   pop   for   me
at   Home   lookes   like
its   Gona   Be   a
fine   liFe
       the
       end

Figure 1c

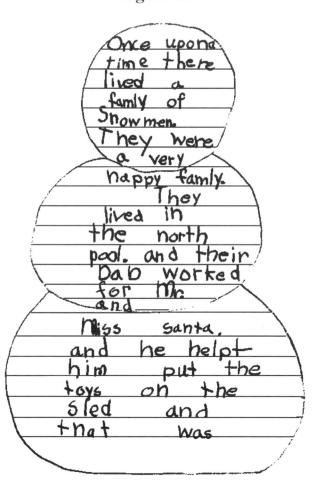

As they become more involved with print, children begin to develop their understanding and mastery of English orthography. In fact, Richard Gentry (1987) has identified five stages of spelling development. What teachers refer to as invented spelling covers the first four of Gentry's stages (see Figure 2).

In the pre-communicative stage, children use alphabetic symbols but show little knowledge of letter-sound correspondence. They may also lack knowledge of the entire alphabet, the distinction between uppercase and lowercase letters, and the left-to-right direction of English orthography.

In the semi-phonetic stage, children begin to understand letter-sound correspondence. That is, they understand that sounds are assigned to letters. At this stage, they often employ rudimentary logic, using single letters, for example, to represent entire words, multiple sounds, and syllables.

Children at the phonetic stage use single letters or groups of letters to represent every speech sound within a word. Although some of their choices do not conform to conventional English spelling, they are systematic and readily interpretable.

Figure 2
Stages of Spelling

Stage	Characteristics	Sample
Pre-communicative	Uses alphabet symbols to represent words without regard to letter-sound correspondence	
Semi-phonetic	Conceptualizes that letters represent sounds in words, but only some of them are represented	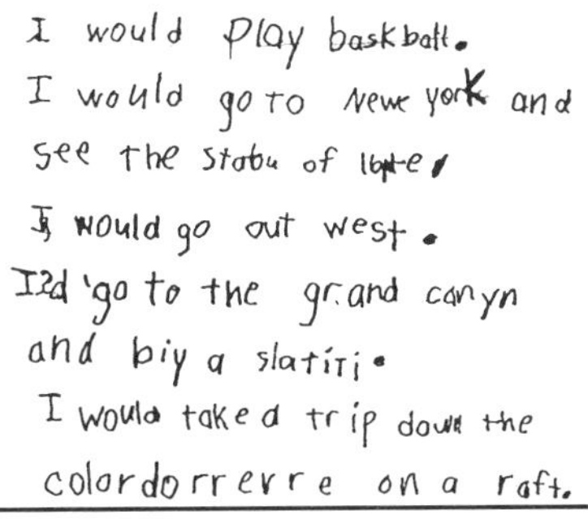
Phonetic	Words are spelled as they sound; all sounds are represented; however, the spelling may be unconventional	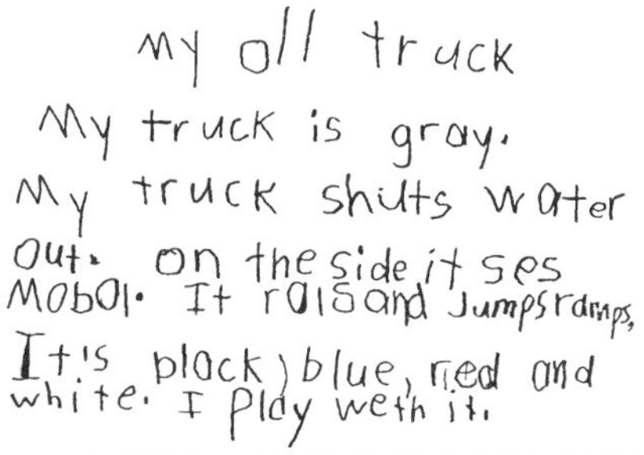
Transitional	Words spelled as they look; visual memory of spelling patterns is apparent	
Standard Spelling	Child spells most of the words correctly	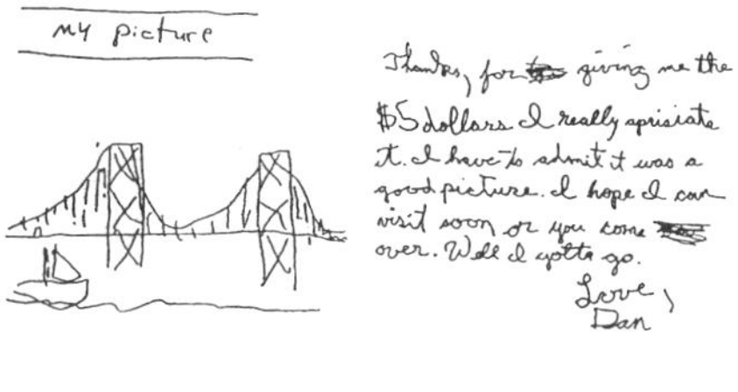

(From Gentry, 1987)

During the transitional stage, children begin to assimilate the standard conventions for representing sounds, moving from a dependence on phonology (sound) for representing words to a reliance on rules governing letter patterns and the structure of words.

In the standard spelling stage, children exhibit a knowledge of the English orthographic system and its basic rules. In particular, they understand how to deal with such things as suffixes, prefixes, silent consonants, and irregular and alternative spellings. Also, children can correctly spell a large number of words and easily recognize incorrect forms.

It is important to note that the changes from one spelling stage to another may be very gradual and that one particular piece of writing may incorporate examples from more than one stage. However, children generally progress through the stages without a great deal of regression or fluctuation.

Learning to spell, then, is not an either-or situation. It is best facilitated by structuring a learning environment where children are allowed and encouraged to use invented spellings and guided in their progression from one stage to another.

Principle #2
Formal Spelling Instruction Should Not Occur Until Students Are Developmentally Ready

In recognition that spelling is a developmental process, students should not be placed in a formal spelling program until they have reached at least the phonetic stage and, ideally, the transitional stage. According to Gentry, by about second grade most children have reached these stages and could profit from some formal instruction. Conversely, children at earlier developmental levels may experience frustration if they are pushed into formal spelling too soon. Therefore, teachers should use their knowledge and understanding of the various stages of spelling development to determine when their second grade classrooms are ready to begin formal instruction. In some classrooms this may be early in the year; for other classrooms it may be late October or November. In still other classrooms formal instruction may not begin until spring.

Principle #3
Writing Should Be the Primary Vehicle for Building Spelling Skills

According to Donald Graves, "Spelling is for Writing." Thus, to teach spelling effectively a teacher must teach writing effectively. It is fairly common knowledge that writing involves a process (see Figure 3).

Figure 3
The Writing Process

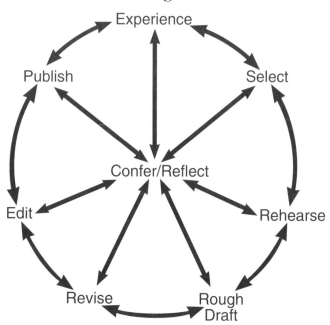

The writing process begins with **experience**. That is, everything we write springs from our experience. Thus, the first step for any author is to tap into his or her experiential base—to identify those ideas and topics he or she considers truly important.

Selecting involves deciding whether an experience is interesting enough to write about. At a more specific level, selecting also involves choosing and narrowing the topic about which to write.

Rehearsal is the part of writing in which information is generated, reviewed, and formulated. Rehearsal might be as structured as gathering information in a library or as unstructured as simply imagining a topic, a character, or a setting. With proper rehearsal, a growing readiness to put pen to paper ensues. At this level of writing, nothing is permanent. Rehearsal is a time to toy with ideas; it is a time to allow the pen or pencil to take the writer in new or unexpected directions.

At some point in time, rehearsal turns into **drafting.** If writing is allowed to progress naturally, this transition occurs quite automatically. Almost without notice, this rehearsal turns into the **rough draft** of a composition. Similarly, the process of drafting turns into the process of **revising**. At a basic level, revising involves going over a piece again and again, moving words and paragraphs, exploring new modes of expression, crossing out, inserting, and deleting. It is a time when the author extends and refines to produce a more coherent, cohesive piece.

During **editing,** a student attends to the formal conventions of the written language. The young author may edit his or her own piece, edit with a partner, or submit his or her piece to the teacher for final editing.

Ultimately, the final expression of the writing process is **publishing**—the celebration of the author's efforts. Publishing also helps provide authentic audiences for students. Below are listed a few ways of publishing student works:

- bookmaking
- pop-up books
- posters
- postcards
- cartoon strips
- big books
- wordless books with tapes
- newscast interviews
- greeting cards
- pantomimes with tape
- advertisements
- flip books with script
- video scripts
- fact files
- plays
- flannel board stories
- pamphlets
- TV production scripts
- readers theater

Publishing or celebrating student work becomes part of the student's experiential base, thus completing the cycle depicted in Figure 3. The student then uses these experiences in future writing efforts.

Throughout the entire cycle of writing, students are constantly **conferring**—responding to each other's work, giving and getting honest reactions and feedback about their writing. In addition to conferring, **reflecting** is central to the writing process. Reflecting helps students' thinking become more critical, creative, and self-regulated within the writing process.

Given that spelling is for writing, where exactly should spelling be reinforced within the writing process? A question that is equally important is: Where should spelling **not** be emphasized within the writing process? We consider this question first.

Correct spelling should not be emphasized during the selecting, rehearsing, drafting, or revising phases of writing. Obviously, you do not think about spelling when you first select a topic. Not so obviously, you do not consider spelling in a systematic way when you rehearse, draft, or even revise a composition. This is because a writer (young or old) has only a limited amount of room in short-term memory. If the writer is using that room to consider how a word is spelled, there will be little or no room left to consider relationships among ideas and the sequencing of ideas. Putting ideas together in such a way that they make sense is the most important aspect of rehearsing, drafting, and revising. Focusing on spelling at these stages, then, can actually inhibit the composing process. Student guesses about how words are spelled (or their invented spellings) allow them to concentrate on what it is they would like to say, thus enhancing the rehearsing, drafting, and revising processes. If too much emphasis is placed on correct spelling at these stages, children may resort to using only words they know how to spell, limiting their creative development. It is important, however, that teachers help students understand that their spellings during these initial writing stages are only **temporary** and that there is an established, acceptable way to spell words.

It is when children reach the stage of **editing** in the writing process that correct spelling becomes an issue. The amount of emphasis placed on correct spelling at this stage is affected by the audience for whom the composition is intended. In other words, the audience for whom the composition will be published dictates the amount of emphasis given to correct spelling.

Publishing involves presenting a composition to an audience, where audience is thought of as a continuum. To illustrate, consider the following representation:

neighbor	teacher	entire	general
or friend		class	public

At one end of the continuum, the audience for a composition is a neighbor or a friend. Farther down the continuum, audience is the teacher. Farther still down the continuum, audience includes the entire class. At the farthest end of the continuum, audience involves the general public outside of the classroom.

Depending on where the audience for a particular work falls on this continuum, correct spelling is more or less important. At the far left of the continuum, where audience involves friends, correct spelling might be considered desirable but not mandatory. Even in the middle of the continuum, where the audience is the teacher, some breaches of conventional spelling might be considered acceptable. However, when the audience for a composition reaches the entire class and beyond (i.e., the general public), correct spelling is essential. The extent to which correct spelling is emphasized, then, is dependent on the audience for whom the writing is intended, as well as the child's developmental level.

Principle #4
Spelling Should Be Taught in
Relationship to Word Meaning

What good does it do a student to know how to spell "antidisestablishmentarianism"? It might impress a few aunts and uncles but it does little for the child's literacy development. To use words effectively in their writing and reading, children must understand their meanings and acquire what some theorists refer to as understanding words as being **labels**. In this context, a word is a label for a set of important distinctions. When you learn or acquire a new label (word), you also acquire a new set of perceptions. For example, before taking a course in astronomy, you might look at the night sky and see only stars. Every little speckle of light looks about

the same. They are all simply "stars." After a few weeks of the course, however, the speckles of light are not all alike. Rather, you begin to see "novas" and "galaxies." You are looking at the same sky but now you have learned an important set of distinctions along with the labels for those distinctions. As the linguist John Condon (1968) says, "When names are learned we see what we had not seen before, for we know what to look for."

Relative to the processes of reading and writing, the importance of word knowledge is fairly obvious. You can't read about something for which you do not know the important words. You simply can't process the information because you don't understand the words. Similarly, you cannot write effectively about something for which you do not have a rich store of words that can express your thoughts. It seems obvious, then, that to teach spelling in isolation from word meaning makes little sense. Stated differently, children should be taught to spell words as they learn the meanings of the words. But just how do we learn new words? To answer this question, consider Figure 4.

Figure 4
The Vocabulary Learning Process

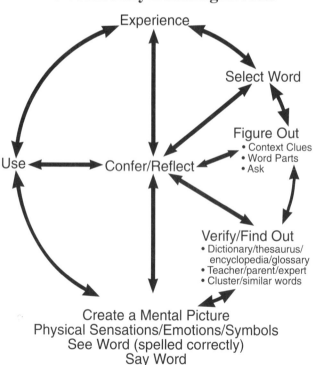

The process of learning a word begins with **experience**. Specifically, words are the organizers for our experiences; they allow us to link one experience with another. Consequently, the first step in the vocabulary learning process is an awareness of how words come from, and directly affect, our experiences. Operationally, this means that students develop a heightened awareness of words in their environment. They begin to notice words more often and to cultivate a curiosity about what words mean.

Based on this heightened awareness, students begin to **select words** of interest for study. Selection is a very important part of the vocabulary learning process; simply stated, you don't need to know all the words you encounter. And as you read, you do not stop to figure out every word you do not know. Rather, you skip some words. Others catch your eye. In other words, you naturally select words of interest and ignore others. Consequently, as part of vocabulary learning students should be continually making choices about which words they would like to learn, selecting ones that are of significant interest to them.

Given the desire to learn about words they have selected, students try to **figure out** their meanings. Students need to be aware that they might already have some knowledge about what these words mean. Is there any context to help them? Have they ever heard the words before or are there any word parts they might be familiar with? They also may simply wish to ask someone what a new word means.

Once an initial guess is made about a word's meaning, the student makes some attempt to **verify** the accuracy of his or her guess. At a very basic level, the student simply keeps his or her eyes open for evidence that would verify the guess. The student may ask a teacher, parent, or expert or look up the word in a dictionary, a glossary, an encyclopedia, or other available reference.

After determining the meaning of a word, the student deepens his or her knowledge of the word by trying to **create a mental picture of the meaning of the word, associating it with physical sensations, emotions, or symbols,** increasing his or her cueing system for storing the word in long-term memory. If the student cannot create a mental representation for the meaning of the word, this might indicate a need to gather more information. While generating a mental representation of the word's meaning, the student practices **saying the word** quietly and **seeing the word** in his or her mind. This is where spelling enters into the vocabulary learning process. It is an important step in the process that occurs after an understanding of a word has developed.

As an understanding of a word develops, students become more comfortable **using** the word in speech and writing. Eventually, their understanding of the new word becomes a part of their experiential base, adding to their knowledge in such a way that they can draw on it to learn other words of interest. Thus, the vocabulary learning process comes full circle.

The vocabulary learning process also involves **conferring** and **reflecting**. Conferring means communicating with others about the word being learned. This may be by asking someone what the word means or clarifying some confusion about the word or comparing other words of similar meaning. Reflecting involves students' thinking about their own thinking—determining what is working well and what is not working well.

The vocabulary learning process, then, is a holistic, integrated act, used by students to learn new words of their own choosing. The message should be quite clear that when students are learning a new word they should take some time to learn how to spell the word. Knowledge of spelling and knowledge of word meaning are two sides of the same coin.

Principle #5
Spelling Instruction Should Involve Student Choice

One of the most powerful principles coming out of the research and theory in learning is that choice is essential to the learning process. The reason is quite simple—motivation. That is, when we have some choice over what we learn we are more motivated. To illustrate, think of a situation in which you chose to learn something and compare it to one in which you were forced to learn something.

Chances are that your learning was much more effective in the situation in which you had a choice. This holds true for spelling instruction also. Students will be more motivated to learn to spell words they have chosen than words provided for them. This does not mean that students should necessarily choose all the words they will learn to spell. Certainly, guidance is required by the teacher to ensure that students master words they will frequently use in their writing or encounter in their reading. An effective spelling program, then, will have a balance between student choice and teacher direction.

How are these five principles integrated into a literature-based approach to spelling? Before answering this question on the nature of formal spelling instruction, we will consider what should occur before formal instruction begins.

Before Formal Instruction Occurs

Because spelling is a developmental process, no formal instruction should occur until students are developmentally ready. This means that students have progressed through the various stages of invented spelling through the transitional stage. As mentioned above, this usually occurs in about second grade. However, it is the teacher who should make the decision as to when formal instruction will begin. This decision should be based on:

- an evaluation of students' writing, using multiple samples.
- the overall interest students have in correct spelling.
- the degree to which students can effectively engage in the editing phase of the writing process.

For more information on determining which stage students are in, see *Spelling for Whole Language Classrooms* (Buchanan, 1989).

Until formal instruction occurs, the teacher can play a significant role in fostering spelling development by engaging in the following activities:

- Help students see themselves as readers and writers and understand that writing helps them as they are learning to spell and that reading reinforces correct spelling.
- Model correct spelling.
- Help children become aware of print and its purpose in their environment.
- Model the process of writing (see Principle #3) and allow children time to write.
- Encourage students to use invented spelling, making guesses about how they think words are spelled, experimenting, and testing and modifying their hypotheses about spelling.

- Help students understand that there are correct ways to spell words that should be considered when preparing a piece for certain audiences.
- Model the vocabulary learning process (see Principle #4) and help students understand the place of spelling within this process.
- Provide students with appropriate sources they can use to help them find the correct spellings of words. If students are using the *Literacy Plus* Word Books, these can be a source for the correct spelling of a word. Other sources include spelling lists, dictionaries, and class spelling charts.
- Provide a setting in which students can interact, discuss, question, and evaluate their spelling ability and growth.
- Provide training for parents in the stages of spelling development and its relationship to the reading and writing processes. Based on their experience in school, many parents are concerned about spelling. However, they may not be aware that spelling is a developmental process and can become discouraged with their child as he or she progresses through the various developmental stages. It should be a high priority of teachers to help parents understand the nature of spelling development and its implications for instruction. Such understanding can be fostered through parent-teacher conferences, back-to-school nights, or written correspondence (see sample of parent letter in Appendix A).

The first step in setting up a formal spelling program is to set aside a daily block of time for spelling development. We suggest that this be approximately 15–20 minutes a day; however, this time frame will certainly fluctuate from session to session. It is helpful to have spelling at a specific time each day so that a predictable routine can be established for children.

The second step is to provide spelling books for each student. In these books, students generate individual spelling lists. In traditional spelling programs students use ready-made lists that allow for neither teacher nor student input. In this program, students generate their own spelling lists; however, as mentioned above, the teacher can control what goes on those lists. Thus, there is **subjectivity with focus**, **flexibility with control**. The words on the lists can come from a number of sources, including the following:

* words from reading
* words from writing
* words from the content areas
* words from the environment
* frequently used words
* words spelled incorrectly from previous spelling lists

Words From Reading

A spelling approach that is literature based should quite obviously rely on the wide reading of students as a source for spelling words. Therefore, as students are reading for pleasure or for course work, they should be on the lookout for words that are of particular interest to them. There are at least two highly effective methods of collecting these words.

* Students can keep small strips of paper in books they are reading. On these they can record words they might like to learn to spell. These words can then be added to a **Spelling Log** (see Figure 5 and **Blackline #1**, located at the back of the book). A Spelling Log is like a holding pen for words students might use on a spelling list. Recording a word in a log means that the student is considering the word for inclusion on a spelling list.
* Teachers and students can keep a classroom record of interesting words from their read-aloud and poetry books. These can be recorded on the chalkboard. If students see particular words that they might like to learn to spell, they can add them to their Spelling Logs.

Words From Writing

Writing is not only a place to use words, it can also be a source of words to include on a spelling list. To use writing as a source of spelling words, students simply identify words they continually misspell and add them to their Spelling Logs. Teachers may wish to help students identify these words during conferences about writing.

Words From the Content Areas

Many of the words students are expected to learn in the content areas can be placed on student spelling lists. This may be especially true when students are involved in thematic units. Using content words in spelling lists helps break down the artificial lines between content areas and provides an interdisciplinary tone to instruction.

Figure 5

Spelling Log

Words From Reading	Words From Writing	Words From Content Areas	Words From Other Sources

▰ Words From the Environment ▰

As students are allowed to select their own spelling words, their interest and enthusiasm for words will increase. As a result, they should become more interested in the many and varied words in their environment. Field trips, excursions, current events, and local happenings become a rich source of words students may desire to use in their writing and therefore may wish to learn to spell.

▰ Frequently Used Words ▰

Frequently used words are a rich source for spelling lists. These words can be listed in two ways. Appendix B lists words by grade level. In all, nine grade levels are covered: kindergarten through eighth grade. All of the words in these lists are frequently used words that students will encounter in their reading and in standardized tests. For a thorough explanation of how these words were selected and how grade levels were assigned, you should read *Literacy Plus: Teacher Reference Book to Words in Semantic Clusters*. Within the grade level in which each word first occurs, the words are ranked by the Standard Frequency Index, or SFI. Again, for a discussion of this index, you should consult the *Teacher Reference Book*. Briefly, though, the higher the SFI, the more common the word. Within grade levels, words are ranked from the most frequently used to the least frequently used. To illustrate, consider the list of kindergarten words in Appendix B. Although all words have a kindergarten designation, the word *the* (which has an SFI of 88.6) is the most frequently encountered word on the list. Conversely, the word *boot* (which has an SFI of 47.5) is the least frequently encountered word on the list. The higher the SFI ranking, the more frequent the word. This frequency index can be helpful to the teacher for making decisions as to which words to select for study.

A second list, *Literacy Plus Spelling Alphabetized Word List* (which is packaged as an optional component of this unit), lists all words from all nine grade levels in alphabetical order. After each word is its grade level and its SFI score. Appendix B and *Literacy Plus Spelling Alphabetized Word List*, then, are useful resources for frequently used words that might be included in students' spelling lists. Specifically, as students select words for their lists, the teacher may wish to encourage or guide them to use some of the frequently used words listed in these sources. The teacher would do this by selecting some words from these lists and allowing students to select from the set provided by the teacher.

▰ Words Spelled Incorrectly From Previous Spelling Lists ▰

The final source of spelling words for student lists is incorrectly spelled words from previous lists. If a student misspells words from one list, these words may be carried over to the next list. It is up to the teacher to determine how many of these words should be included on a subsequent list.

As you can tell from the foregoing, helping students construct their individual spelling lists is a key aspect of formal spelling instruction. A number of questions are frequently asked about this process.

How many words should be on the list, and what sources will be used?

These decisions are controlled entirely by the teacher. Second grade students will obviously have fewer words in their vocabulary lists than fifth grade students. The number of words and the sources can vary from week to week and from grade level to grade level. For example, one week the teacher may ask students to create lists that have ten words; the next week he or she might ask them to create lists of fifteen words; the next list might have eight words, and so on. In addition to the number of words on a list, the teacher can specify the various sources to be used in constructing the lists. Figure 6 shows one possible list of sources.

Figure 6

Name _____ Spelling List # _____

Date _____ Test Date _____

#	Source	Word	✓	Cluster	Show You Know
1	Math				
2	Math				
3	Writing				
4	Writing				
5	Reading				
6	Reading				
7	Science				
8	Science				
9	Social Studies				
10	Social Studies				

Figure 7

Name _____ Spelling List # _____

Date _____ Test Date _____

#	Source	Word	✓	Cluster	Show You Know
1	Reading				
2	Reading				
3	Reading				
4	Reading				
5	Frequently Used				
6	Frequently Used				
7	Frequently Used				
8	Frequently Used				
9					
10					

Here the teacher has specified that there will be ten words on the spelling list. Two words should come from mathematics, two from student writing, two from student wide reading, and so on. However, for the next list, the teacher might decide that there will be only eight spelling words and that the sources will be entirely different from those on the previous list (see Figure 7).

Here the teacher has specified that four words should come from students' wide reading. The remaining four words will be selected by students from a list of frequently used words the teacher writes on the board. That is, the teacher would consult Appendix B or the *Literacy Plus Spelling Alphabetized Word List*, select about ten frequently used words, and list them on the board. Students would then select four words from this list to include in their individual spelling lists.

When do students make their lists?

New spelling lists are usually begun each Monday during the time that has been allotted for spelling. This does not necessarily mean that students construct a new list each week. Sometimes the words on a specific list may be very complex, in which case the teacher and the students might want more time on that particular list: ten days or two weeks.

How individualized are the lists?

This is also up to the discretion of the teacher. For one spelling list, the teacher might give students total freedom to select the words as long as they stay within the source guidelines that have been established (e.g., two words from social studies, two from reading, and so on). Another variation might be that the teacher (after identifying the number of words and their source) might provide a list of several words from each identified source. Students would then select words from the various lists the teacher has provided. For example, a teacher might put ten frequently used words on the chalkboard and ask students to select two of them, ten words from social studies and ask students to select two from that list, and so on.

Finally, on occasion, the teacher might decide that there are certain words from a particular source that the entire class needs to know. All students would then be required to include those words in their spelling lists. In short, there is a great deal of flexibility as to the extent to which spelling lists are individualized.

What about second and third grade classrooms? Are all of their lists individualized?

As formal spelling instruction begins, the teacher may wish to limit the extent to which spelling lists are individualized until students develop an understanding of what is expected of them and how to select words.

To begin with, lists might be prepared by the entire class. Next, the teacher may have students develop their lists in small groups. Students could then develop lists as partners and finally as individuals. It also is advisable to offer a variety of these groupings throughout the year, not only in the second and third grades but also in the intermediate grades.

Will students pick words that are too easy or that they already know how to spell?

On the contrary, students seem to pick words that are too difficult. Students should be reminded that the words they have selected for spelling should be words they will be using in their writing. If their selected words are ones they would hardly ever use, they may wish to select others that may be more commonly used in their writing and that they do not know how to spell.

Can students help each other select words for their lists?

Absolutely; in fact, teachers should encourage such interaction. Allowing students to work with spelling partners is recommended. These partners can be changed at regular intervals, allowing students to interact with as many different members of the class as possible.

Where do students write these lists?

An individual spelling booklet (*My Spelling and Word Meaning Book*) is provided for each child. Each book contains forms on which students enter the source of the words to be selected and the actual words selected (see Figure 8). For each word, there is also a space labeled "Cluster" and one labeled "Show You Know" (these are explained under the next two questions). Finally, each form also contains a space for the student's name, the date the list was initiated, and the date on which a test will occur.

What does "Cluster" mean?

The column in each spelling list labeled "Cluster" is to help students make connections with words they already know. It simply means relating a word that has been selected to a bigger group of words, i.e., a cluster of words. For example, if a student selected the word "screwdriver," he or she might decide that it belongs in the general cluster of words called "Tools." Thus, the student would write "tools" under the "Cluster" column next to that word. This act of categorizing each word makes students think deeply about the meanings of the words they wish to learn to spell.

Although this spelling program can be used in isolation, it is meant to be used in conjunction with the complete *Literacy Plus* approach to language arts development. Again, to understand that program you should read the *Literacy Plus Teacher Guide*. A central focus of that program is vocabulary development through the use of semantic clusters. Within the *Literacy Plus* approach, students are provided with individual Word Books. The Word Books are organized into semantic clusters— groups of words whose meanings are in some way related. In all, there are 61 major clusters of related words, which are listed in Figure 9.

The *Literacy Plus* Word Books have a dual purpose. One is to provide students with a list of target words for their consideration and study. Consequently, the words listed in the Word Books are those that students will frequently encounter. They were taken from student textbooks, leisure reading

Figure 8

Name _____ Spelling List # _____

Date _____ Test Date _____

#	Source	Word	✓	Cluster	Show You Know
1					
2					
3					
4					
5					
6					
7					
8					
9					
10					

Literacy Plus
Copyright © Zaner-Bloser, Inc.

materials, and standardized tests. Another purpose of the Word Books is to provide students with a structure for associating new words gleaned from their wide reading with words they already know. In this way, the Word Books become highly personalized; they become a reflection of each student's interests and preferences. Hence, the Word Books have a dual function: they expose students in a loose but focused way to words they should know, and they provide a structure that allows them to record and study words they select from their own experiences with language. For students who are using the *Literacy Plus* Word Books, then, the notion of identifying the cluster to which a word belongs will be quite natural and will go hand in hand with other vocabulary development activities.

For those classrooms in which students are not using the *Literacy Plus* Word Books, the teacher may wish to consider placing the poster showing the appropriate level of cluster headings on the wall to help students see how to complete the cluster portion of their spelling lists.

Figure 9
The 61 Super-Clusters

1. Occupations/Pursuits
2. Types of Motion/Activity
3. Size/Quantity/Weight
4. Animals
5. Feelings/Attitudes
6. Food Types/Meal Types
7. Time
8. Machines/Engines/Tools
9. Types of People
10. Communication
11. Transportation
12. Mental Actions/Thinking
13. Human Traits/Behavior
14. Location/Direction
15. Literature/Writing
16. Water/Liquids
17. Clothing
18. Places Where People Might Live/Dwell
19. Noises/Sounds
20. Land/Terrain
21. Dwellings/Shelters
22. Materials and Building
23. The Human Body
24. Vegetation
25. Groups of Things
26. Value/Correctness
27. Similarity/Dissimilarity
28. Money/Finance
29. Soil/Metal/Rock
30. Rooms/Furnishing/Parts of Dwellings/Buildings
31. Attitudinals
32. Shapes/Dimensions
33. Destructive and Helpful Actions
34. Sports/Recreation
35. Language
36. Ownership/Possession
37. Disease/Health
38. Light
39. Causality
40. Weather
41. Cleanliness/Uncleanliness
42. Popularity/Familiarity
43. Physical Traits of People
44. Touching/Grabbing Actions
45. Pronouns
46. Contractions
47. Entertainment/The Arts
48. Walking/Running Actions
49. Mathematics
50. Auxiliary/Helping Verbs
51. Events
52. Temperature/Fire
53. Images/Perceptions
54. Life/Survival
55. Conformity/Complexity
56. Difficulty/Danger
57. Texture/Durability
58. Color
59. Chemicals
60. Facial Expressions/Actions
61. Electricity/Particles of Matter

What does "Show You Know" mean?

The **Show You Know** portion of student spelling lists requires students to represent the meanings of words they have selected. Like identifying the cluster a word belongs to, the "show you know" activity reinforces the importance of knowing the meaning of words, not just their spellings. There are a number of ways students can fill in the Show You Know columns of their spelling lists.
- draw a picture or a symbol
- think of a similar word
- create a sentence
- write a description in their own words
- list examples of the word

To illustrate, Figure 10 contains an example of each of these ways a student might "show you know" the meaning of words.

Filling in the Cluster and Show You Know columns of the spelling lists does not have to be a tedious exercise for students. Students should be encouraged to interact as much as possible as they fill in these two columns. Also, the teacher might decide that students do not have to fill in these two columns for **every** word on their spelling lists. Instead the teacher might ask students to fill in these two columns for a certain number of words in a given spelling list. The teacher might vary the ways in which students fill in these two columns by:
- having students work together in groups of three or four and timing them to see which group can complete the Cluster and Show You Know sections first.
- walking around the classroom, going from student to student, asking if they know what a word means and the clusters it might belong to. This interaction would be done instead of filling in the Cluster and Show You Know columns.
- having students talk as a class about words they are unsure of.
- asking students to take their words home and have their parents help them.
- inviting older children from other classrooms to aid younger children in filling in the Cluster and Show You Know sections.

When do students fill in the spaces for Cluster and Show You Know?

Students may do this during the allotted spelling period or they may take their spelling lists home and have parents or siblings help them fill in this information.

Does preparing these lists take a long time?

Preparing individualized spelling lists is a more thoughtful and intensive approach than that taken in traditional programs. However, it does not take as long as one might think, especially when students become familiar with the process.

How do you check to see whether students have recorded words on their lists correctly?

It obviously is critical that students correctly record words they have selected on their spelling lists. After students have made their selection of words, we suggest that teachers, classroom aides, or parents take a few moments to check the lists. A small check mark can be placed beside the word if it is spelled correctly. If there is no check mark, students will know that they need to find the correct spelling of the word (see Figure 11).

When are students tested on their words?

Again, it is up to the teacher to decide when tests will take place. Commonly, tests occur every Friday; however, if the words selected for a particular week are fairly difficult, the teacher may decide not to have a test for two weeks.

Figure 10

Name ___Sue C.___   Spelling List # ___4___

Date ___Oct. 6___   Test Date ___Oct. 10___

#	Source	Word	✓	Cluster	Show You Know
1	Science	materials	✓	materials	supplies
2	Science	science	✓	human body	weather energy physics chemistry biology
3	Math	trapezoid		mathematics	
4	Math	mathematics	✓	mathematics	addition subtraction multiplication division
5	Social Studies	geography	✓	occupations	study of the earth
6	Social Studies	United States	✓	live or dwell	The U.S. is made up of 50 states.
7	Writing	ambushed	✓	Destructive Actions	suddenly attacked
8	Writing	penitentiary	✓	dwellings	jail or prison
9	Reading	ominous	✓	destructive actions	dangerous
10	Reading	glamorous	✓	clothing	beautiful
11	Previous Spelling	porpoise	✓	animals	an underwater animal found in the ocean
12					

Literacy Plus
Copyright © Zaner-Bloser, Inc.

19

Figure 11

Name **Sue C.** Spelling List # **5**

Date **Oct. 13** Test Date **Oct. 17**

#	Source	Word	✓	Cluster	Show You Know
1	Social Studies	Colorado	✓		
2	Social Studies	elavation			
3	Social Studies	resource	✓		
4	Reading	technical	✓		
5	Reading	apprentice	✓		
6	Reading	education	✓		
7	Math	diameter	✓		
8	Math	circumference	✓		
9	Writing	archatect			
10	Writing	career	✓		
11					
12					

Literacy Plus
Copyright © Zaner-Bloser, Inc.

Included in *My Spelling and Word Meaning Book* are forms on which students complete their tests (see Figure 12). The tests are administered by the students, working in pairs. Partners exchange their individual lists. One partner gives the words while the other partner writes each word. It is important to realize that during this stage of testing students do not fill out the Show You Know column of the spelling test. Rather, they simply write the word in the column labeled "Word" as they would in a regular spelling test. When both partners have written their words, they simultaneously complete the rest of the test, which involves filling out the Show You Know column for each word.

Again, the teacher decides how much emphasis to place on this portion of the test. One week students may be expected to fill in the Show You Know portion for each word on the test. Another week the teacher may ask for a Show You Know for some of the words.

The tests then can be scored in a variety of ways. The teacher may wish to score each one him or herself or even enlist the help of a classroom aide or parent volunteer. Or each student might score his or her own test. Students do so by comparing what they wrote on their spelling test with what they have written on their individual spelling lists. In any case, a point is given for each word spelled correctly and a point for each correct Show You Know. A percentage score is calculated and a record of this score is kept.

How do you know if students are using their spelling words in their writing?

One way is simply to ask students during individual writing conferences to identify words they have used that came from their spelling lists. Another way is to have students highlight words from their spelling lists in their rough drafts so they can be easily identified.

Figure 12

Name _____

Spelling Test # _____ Date _____

#	Word	✓	Show You Know	✓
1				
2				
3				
4				
5				
6				
7				
8				
9				
10				

Applying Strategies and Rules

When students are not constructing their spelling lists or taking spelling tests, they should be presented with strategies and rules to apply to their spelling lists. Strategies should also be modeled for students. As students develop a repertoire of strategies, they should then select the ones they will use to study the words on their spelling lists.

Some strategies might be very specific in their use. For example, students may need a strategy for helping them spell while writing (see Figure 13).

Figure 13

A Strategy for Spelling a Word While Writing

1. Try to spell the word two or three different ways, writing down each attempt.

2. Look at the various spellings for the word. Which ones look wrong? Which ones look right?

3. If you think one looks correct, use it. If you want to be sure, go to a source such as a dictionary or thesaurus.

4. See the correct spelling in your mind.

Or students may need a strategy to help them copy words correctly from a text to their spelling list (see Figure 14).

Still other students may need a strategy for helping them study a word on their own (see Figure 15).

Figure 14

A Strategy for Copying a Word From a Text

1. Look carefully at the word.

2. Notice each letter.

3. Write the word on your paper.

4. Check the first letter of the word in the text.

5. Look at the first letter in your word. If it is the same, place a dot under that letter. If it isn't, change it to the correct letter.

6. Continue this process until all the letters in your word have been checked.

Figure 15

A Strategy for Studying a Word

1. Look carefully at the word.

2. Say each letter in the word.

3. Close your eyes and see each letter in your mind.

4. Say the letters out loud.

5. Look at the word to see if you were correct.

6. Write the word down.

7. Check to see whether you wrote it down correctly.

8. If you were incorrect, repeat steps 1 to 7.

Strategies may also be presented in a gamelike format. For example, Figure 16 contains a list of gamelike strategies for studying spelling words.

Figure 16

Game Strategies for Studying Spelling Words

- Create a picture using the word.

- Write each letter of the word on a separate card. Then mix the cards up and see if you can place them in the correct order.

- Have practice tests with a partner.

- Create a crossword puzzle with the words on your list.

- Create a riddle or mnemonic device for remembering the word.

(For more information on games for spelling see *Literacy Plus Games for Vocabulary and Spelling*.)

In addition to spelling strategies, a teacher should present students with some spelling rules. In doing this, teachers should consider the research of Theodore Clymer (1963) who found that only 18 out of 45 spelling rules were truly useful. Similarly, Lillie Smith Davis (1972) found that only nine spelling generalizations apply 100 percent of the time. These are:

- When **c** and **h** are next to each other they make only one sound (*torch*).
- When the letter **c** is followed by **o** or **a** the sound of **k** is likely to be heard (*vacant*).
- When **ght** is seen in a word, the **gh** is silent (*light*).
- When a word begins with **kn**, the **k** is silent (*knee*).
- When a word begins with **wr**, the **w** is silent (*wreck*).
- When a word ends in **ck**, it has the same last sound as in *look* (*truck*).
- When **ture** is the final syllable in a word, it is unaccented (*venture*).
- When **tion** is the final syllable in a word, it is unaccented (*election*).
- When the first vowel element in a word is followed by **th**, **ch**, or **sh**, these symbols are not broken when the word is divided into syllables and may go with either the first or second syllable (*feathers*).

Steve Graham and Lamoine Miller (1979) suggest that spelling rules be limited to the following:

- the use of capital letters to begin proper nouns and most adjectives formed from proper nouns
- rules for adding suffixes (changing **y** to **i**, dropping final silent **e**, doubling the final consonant)
- the use of periods in writing abbreviations
- the use of the apostrophe to show possession
- that the letter **q** is followed by **u** in common English words
- that English words do not end in **v**

Since students will be taking regular spelling tests and receiving percentage scores, they can use this information to assess their spelling development. In the back of *My Spelling and Word Meaning Book* is a personal chart on which they can graph their spelling progress from test to test (see Figure 17). After students have scored their tests, they can record their scores on these charts. At the end of each month during conferencing, the teacher and student can then discuss any patterns that may be evident from the chart and record the student's progress on the Cumulative Spelling Chart (see Figure 18 and **Blackline #2**) for parent conferences and for the cumulative portfolio.

Teachers might also take regular samples of students' writing to help evaluate spelling progress. A composition may even be given a spelling score. For example, a writing sample of 35 words could be taken. Of these 35 words, 27 words were spelled correctly, giving an overall score of 79%. Over a period of time, these scores can be evaluated to see if students are making progress. Teachers, however, must be cautious in selecting writing samples. Obviously, a finished version of something should contain fewer errors than a rough draft. Therefore, writing samples used to evaluate spelling progress should all be the products of the same phase of the writing process.

Students should also be encouraged to assess their own progress. A child's overall feelings about his or her growth in spelling, the strategies that he or she is using, and the needs he or she perceives are invaluable information.

■ Linking Spelling to Vocabulary ■

If students use the vocabulary learning process described in Principle #4 of this unit, they will have a natural connection between vocabulary development and spelling development. As they learn the spellings of new words, they also learn their meanings. As they learn the meanings of new words, they also learn how to spell them. In fact, the comprehensive *Literacy Plus* program recommends the use of a vocabulary workshop separated from spelling periods. The vocabulary workshop is merely a block of time set aside to concentrate on vocabulary growth. A workshop commonly will include a mini-lesson, which demonstrates a specific strategy, skill, or convention important to vocabulary development; an activity period, in which students may work on vocabulary activities; and a sharing period, in which students may discuss new insights, raise questions, or simply share experiences. Since students are discovering meaning for their spelling words, these words may often be used in the vocabulary workshop. Similarly, many words students learn during vocabulary workshops can be used in spelling lists. For a detailed discussion of the vocabulary workshop, see the *Literacy Plus Teacher Guide*.

Figure 17

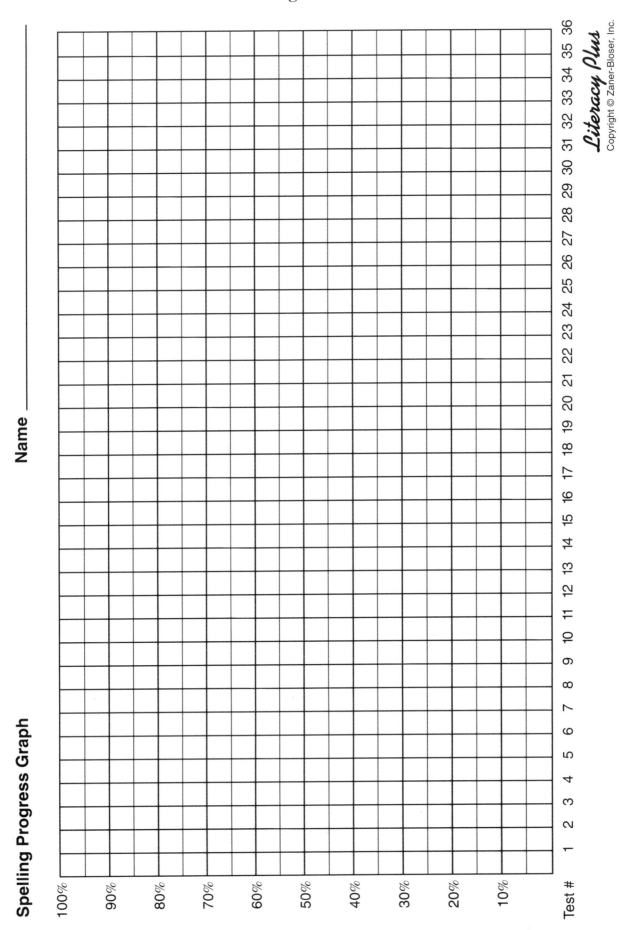

Name _____

Spelling Progress Graph

100% 90% 80% 70% 60% 50% 40% 30% 20% 10%

Test # 1 2 3 4 5 6 7 8 9 10 11 12 13 14 15 16 17 18 19 20 21 22 23 24 25 26 27 28 29 30 31 32 33 34 35 36

26

Figure 18
Cumulative Spelling Chart

Name _____

Teacher _____ Year _____

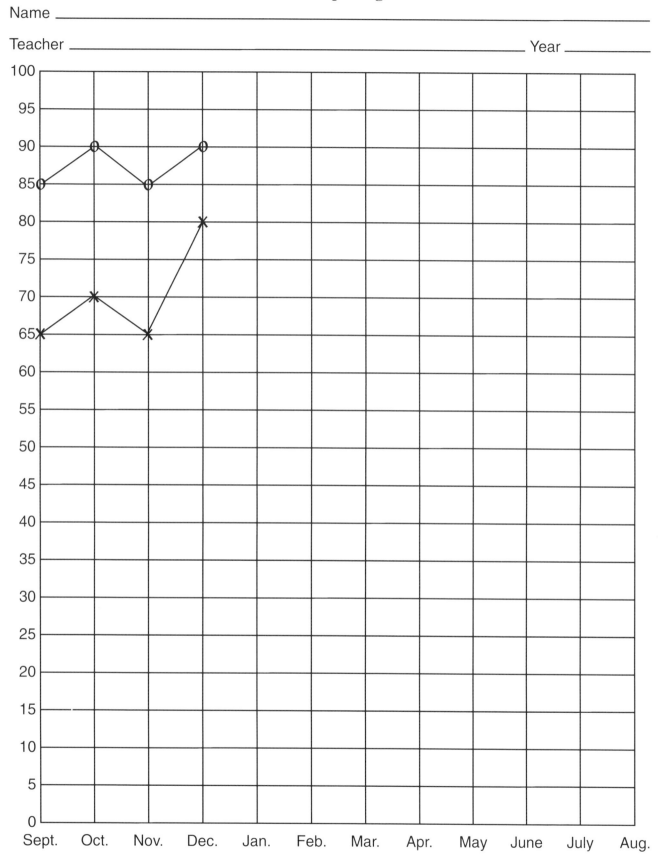

X—X Spelling scores
O—O Show You Know scores

Seeing the Whole Picture

Let's Wrap It Up

In this book we have presented the inner workings of the *Literacy Plus* approach to spelling. Although it might appear complex, it actually is quite simple. Basically, using this program includes the following steps:

1. Establish a 15- to 20-minute period each day for spelling instruction.
2. Provide *My Spelling and Word Meaning Book* for students. We also recommend that the *Literacy Plus* Word Books be used in conjunction with *My Spelling and Word Meaning Book*.
3. On a systematic basis, have students construct individual spelling lists. This involves the following process:
   - Decide how many words will be on the spelling list and tell the students.
   - Identify the sources from which students will select words and tell the students.
   - Identify the number and sources of words that will be left up to student choice and tell the students.
   - Provide guidance as students construct their lists and check to see that the words on their lists are spelled correctly.
4. Present and model the use of spelling strategies and rules.
5. Coordinate the administration of the spelling tests.
6. Have students record their spelling scores in their spelling books.
7. Hold periodic conferences with students about their progress in spelling.
8. Systematically integrate the study of spelling with vocabulary development, reading, and writing.

References

Buchanan, Ethel. *Spelling for Whole Language Classrooms*. Winnipeg: Whole Language Consultants Ltd., 1989.

Clymer, Theodore. "The Utility of Phonic Generalizations in the Primary Grades." *Reading Teacher*, XIV (January 1963) 252–258.

Condon, John. *Semantics and Communication*. New York: Macmillan, 1968.

Davis, Lillie Smith. "The Applicability of Phonemic Generalizations to Selected Spelling Programs." *Elementary English*, XLIX (1972) 706–713.

Gentry, J. Richard. *Spel...Is a Four-Letter Word*. Portsmouth, N.H.: Heinemann, 1987.

Graham, Steve, and Lamoine Miller. "Spelling Research and Practice: A Unified Approach." *Focus on Exceptional Children*, XII (October 1979) 1–16.

Letter to Parents

Dear Parents:

The purpose of this letter is to provide you with information about the approach we are using for the teaching of spelling during this school year. We have had a number of requests for this information and many have expressed an interest in knowing how parents can support what we are doing. This is particularly encouraging, as we are constantly seeking ways to help students become better spellers as well as to heighten their awareness of the importance of spelling accurately in all of their work.

Structure of the Program

Some aspects of our spelling program will be similar to what students have experienced in the past. They will receive a list on most Mondays and a spelling test will be given later in the week. However, rather than just receiving a list of unconnected words and memorizing how they are spelled, students will be filling in a sheet that includes the following columns:

Source	Word	Cluster	Show You Know

Source: For each word listed in the **Word** column, the teacher will provide a **Source.** This tells the student that words are selected for a reason: they are words that students have encountered or will be using in their studies. For example, the source for three of the words on the list might be Science, which means the words are important to the science unit the class has been studying. Another source might be Writing, which means the word has been frequently misspelled in recent writing assignments. Examples of sources that will appear in this column throughout this year are as follows:

1. words from students' reading
2. words students are misspelling in their writing
3. words from content area studies (science, social studies, etc.)
4. words of interest
5. words that appear frequently in materials at their grade level
6. words from previous spelling tests

Word: The spelling list of words for the week will be listed here, spelled correctly. To begin with, the teacher may provide the words for students to study. Eventually, however, teachers will provide the source and then allow students some freedom in selecting their own words that might be interesting, troublesome, or useful to them. Student-selected words will be closely monitored by the teacher, but allowing this freedom will communicate to students that different students need to study different words. The goal is to develop in students the habit of learning to spell words that are important to them.

Cluster: This refers to a specific name or title given to words whose meanings are somewhat related. This ties the spelling program to a specific vocabulary program we are using. Your child should be able to explain the meaning of "Cluster."

Show You Know: In this column, students will be asked to show that they understand the meanings of the words they are learning to spell. It does not make sense to study the spelling of a word if they do not understand its meaning well enough to use it in their own work. This does not mean students need precise, dictionary definitions. They will be learning that there are a number of ways to "Show You Know" a word: write synonyms, use the word meaningfully in a sentence, draw a picture, give examples of the word, etc.

Schedule

On most Mondays, students will complete the Source and Word columns. Through the week, they will be studying the spelling of the words, learning strategies for remembering how to spell words correctly, and finding the meanings of any unfamiliar words on the list. The emphasis of the test will be on their ability to spell the words correctly, but some words will also be selected for them to "show they know" the meanings. A sample spelling sheet is attached so that you will know what to expect each week.

Your Support

If you are in the habit of helping your child study for spelling tests, we hope you will also discuss the words to determine whether he or she knows why the word is on the list and what the word means. Discussing the words on the list with your child will help us communicate that spelling is part of learning to use a word correctly, not just a subject in school.

If you have further questions, we encourage you to ask your child to explain the program to you. It is important that they understand not only **what** to do but **why** they are studying spelling in this manner. If you are confused or have any feedback for us, please call at any time.

Sincerely yours,

Appendix B
Standard Frequency Index Listed by Grade

Kindergarten

the	88.6	me	69.9
of	84.5	too	69.8
and	84.2	day	69.7
a	83.9	look	69.5
to	83.7	come	69.2
in	82.9	work	69.2
is	80.7	here	69.0
you	79.8	take	69.0
that	79.7	put	68.7
it	79.6	away	68.5
he	79.2	say	68.3
for	78.9	name	68.0
on	78.5	big	67.9
are	78.3	food	66.7
as	78.0	boy	66.6
with	77.7	story	65.9
they	77.2	sun	65.5
at	76.7	play	64.9
from	76.5	car	64.8
this	76.5	red	64.5
I	76.4	book	64.3
or	76.0	run	64.3
by	75.9	dog	63.6
but	75.6	green	63.5
not	75.6	yes	63.5
what	75.3	am	63.0
all	75.2	stop	63.0
we	74.9	ball	62.9
can	74.6	blue	62.9
there	74.6	rain	62.3
an	74.5	bird	61.6
your	74.4	fun	60.8
do	73.9	yellow	60.5
will	73.9	cat	60.2
up	73.8	sit	59.9
out	73.7	brown	59.7
she	73.6	gray	59.2
them	73.6	hat	59.2
then	73.6	sing	58.7
so	73.5	hill	58.6
into	73.1	wet	58.2
no	72.1	bell	57.4
see	72.1	sad	57.2
its	71.5	cow	56.7
who	71.4	pet	55.3
did	71.2	yours	54.6
my	71.2	zoo	53.6
down	71.1	pin	52.6
little	70.6	kitten	51.7
get	70.3	puppy	51.0
back	70.2	fan	50.4
go	70.0	boot	47.5
good	70.0		

First Grade

was	78.7	three	69.2
his	77.3	word	69.2
be	76.6	because	69.1
have	76.4	does	69.1
one	75.9	even	69.1
had	75.6	part	69.1
were	75.1	why	68.8
when	74.9	help	68.7
which	74.3	again	68.5
their	74.0	off	68.5
if	73.9	old	68.5
about	73.8	tell	68.4
how	73.8	small	68.2
many	73.5	still	68.1
some	73.5	should	68.0
these	73.3	home	67.9
would	73.3	give	67.8
other	73.2	under	67.6
has	73.0	last	67.5
more	72.9	read	67.5
her	72.7	us	67.5
like	72.7	left	67.4
two	72.7	next	67.2
him	72.5	saw	67.2
could	72.1	both	67.1
time	72.1	those	67.1
make	71.9	always	67.0
than	71.8	house	67.0
first	71.7	don't	66.9
been	71.6	school	66.9
now	71.4	want	66.9
people	71.3	until	66.8
over	71.2	feet	66.7
only	71.1	once	66.6
way	71.1	side	66.6
find	70.9	four	66.4
water	70.8	head	66.4
long	70.7	kind	66.4
after	70.6	live	66.4
very	70.6	far	66.3
just	70.4	hand	66.3
know	70.3	need	66.3
where	70.3	high	66.2
before	70.1	light	66.2
much	70.1	mother	66.2
new	70.0	year	66.2
our	70.0	father	66.1
write	70.0	let	66.1
man	69.9	night	66.0
right	69.6	picture	66.0
also	69.4	second	65.9
think	69.4	soon	65.9
must	69.2	white	65.8

First Grade

hard	65.7	dry	62.5	song	59.8	tie	56.2
near	65.7	game	62.5	ring	59.7	paint	56.0
paper	65.7	leave	62.5	love	59.5	sorry	56.0
best	65.6	begin	62.4	send	59.5	dream	55.9
better	65.6	doing	62.4	glad	59.4	cage	55.8
today	65.6	ice	62.4	lady	59.4	cook	55.8
sure	65.5	third	62.4	happen	59.3	joy	55.8
thing	65.4	snow	62.3	pick	59.3	rocket	55.8
hear	65.3	lay	62.2	row	59.1	cap	55.7
room	65.1	sky	62.2	sheep	59.1	chicken	55.7
sea	65.1	wild	62.2	fit	59.0	jet	55.7
learn	65.0	boat	62.1	bread	58.9	Saturday	55.7
city	64.9	care	62.0	rope	58.9	chain	55.5
five	64.9	glass	62.0	nine	58.8	duck	55.5
money	64.9	hour	62.0	truck	58.7	gentle	55.5
morning	64.8	tiny	62.0	spot	58.6	balloon	55.4
turn	64.7	alone	61.9	cloth	58.5	rabbit	55.4
cut	64.6	walk	61.9	string	58.5	snake	55.4
fish	64.5	ask	61.8	nice	58.3	Sunday	55.4
black	64.4	fall	61.8	feed	58.2	pool	55.3
eat	64.4	friend	61.8	gun	58.2	elephant	55.2
open	64.3	job	61.8	star	58.2	mouse	55.2
cold	64.2	map	61.8	surprise	58.2	miss	55.1
table	64.2	window	61.8	camp	58.1	pan	55.1
tree	64.2	farm	61.7	jump	58.1	pony	55.1
front	64.1	week	61.7	angry	58.0	mail	55.0
inside	64.1	bed	61.6	bag	58.0	pen	55.0
ago	64.0	color	61.6	breakfast	58.0	hang	54.7
close	64.0	fly	61.5	coat	58.0	fifth	54.5
early	64.0	teacher	61.5	dress	58.0	dish	54.3
I'll	64.0	happy	61.4	proud	58.0	dot	54.2
nothing	64.0	baby	61.2	bus	57.7	hello	54.1
add	63.9	grass	61.2	drawing	57.7	horn	54.1
call	63.9	plane	61.2	leg	57.6	shoe	54.1
draw	63.9	street	61.2	wagon	57.6	unhappy	54.1
behind	63.8	child	61.1	forget	57.5	wing	54.1
letter	63.8	maybe	61.1	fourth	57.5	doll	53.8
mean	63.6	eye	61.0	lake	57.5	monkey	53.8
six	63.6	milk	61.0	nest	57.5	policeman	53.8
fire	63.5	seven	61.0	push	57.5	toy	53.8
ready	63.5	trip	61.0	barn	57.4	happily	53.7
hot	63.4	wish	61.0	clock	57.4	spin	53.7
person	63.4	woman	61.0	lunch	57.3	shout	53.6
town	63.4	late	60.9	spell	57.3	silly	53.6
fast	63.3	pay	60.9	apple	57.2	trap	53.6
ten	63.3	sleep	60.9	egg	57.2	wolf	53.6
box	63.2	store	60.9	plate	57.2	Friday	53.5
can't	63.2	won't	60.8	airplane	57.1	pig	53.4
horse	63.2	edge	60.7	bowl	57.1	button	53.3
start	63.2	eight	60.7	cry	57.1	penny	53.3
class	63.1	party	60.5	fat	57.1	calf	53.2
talk	63.0	bad	60.4	hurry	57.1	ant	53.1
dark	62.9	tail	60.4	shop	57.1	cart	53.1
girl	62.9	wait	60.4	funny	57.0	gay	53.1
road	62.9	corner	60.3	laugh	56.9	goat	53.1
animal	62.7	guess	60.3	pencil	56.9	pop	53.0
moon	62.7	huge	60.3	cup	56.7	god	52.9
summer	62.7	ride	60.3	fur	56.6	bush	52.8
everyone	62.6	sign	60.3	thank	56.6	promise	52.8
follow	62.6	afraid	60.0	pocket	56.5	ribbon	52.8
winter	62.6	pull	60.0	lion	56.4	bee	52.7
bring	62.5	fresh	59.9	birthday	56.3	honey	52.5
		train	59.9	cake	56.3	turtle	52.5
		king	59.8	whale	56.3	tiger	52.4

Monday	52.3	hen	50.9	toss	49.5		
painting	52.2	butterfly	50.8	clown	49.2		
print	52.2	hi	50.6	drink	48.8	sock	44.8
toys	52.1	bean	50.5	yell	48.7	papa	44.5
sixth	52.0	Thursday	50.5	Wednesday	48.6	frog	44.2
bike	51.8	Tuesday	50.5	jam	48.3	mailman	43.6
seal	51.7	hop	50.4	peanut	48.2	page	42.9
sled	51.7	eighth	50.2	ninth	48.0	mom	42.2
squirrel	51.6	tenth	50.2	fireman	47.5	crayon	41.2
lamb	51.1	ham	49.8	nap	47.0	bunny	36.7
kite	51.0	seventh	49.5	cookie	46.8		

Second Grade

each	73.8	try	65.5	warm	62.7	mouth	61.1
most	70.3	young	65.5	beautiful	62.6	step	61.1
through	70.2	answer	65.2	beginning	62.6	choose	61.0
any	69.8	point	65.0	deep	62.6	north	61.0
same	69.7	top	65.0	heavy	62.6	strange	61.0
around	69.4	himself	64.9	everything	62.5	oil	60.9
another	69.3	toward	64.9	shall	62.5	trouble	60.9
place	69.0	body	64.7	watch	62.5	catch	60.8
such	69.0	family	64.7	carry	62.4	speak	60.8
well	69.0	I'm	64.7	floor	62.4	age	60.7
different	68.6	later	64.7	possible	62.3	minute	60.7
number	68.5	upon	64.7	real	62.3	soft	60.7
great	68.4	done	64.6	easy	62.2	forest	60.6
every	68.2	door	64.6	size	62.2	meet	60.6
found	68.1	face	64.6	someone	62.2	record	60.6
between	68.0	group	64.6	center	62.1	he's	60.5
air	67.7	move	64.6	field	62.1	I've	60.5
line	67.7	half	64.5	question	62.1	south	60.5
set	67.7	true	64.5	stay	62.1	ahead	60.4
own	67.6	short	64.4	wide	62.1	pair	60.4
never	67.5	ground	64.3	else	62.0	practice	60.4
end	67.4	really	64.2	foot	62.0	sand	60.4
might	67.3	grow	63.9	gold	62.0	test	60.4
while	67.3	idea	63.9	low	62.0	wrong	60.4
below	67.2	cannot	63.8	plant	62.0	forward	60.3
sound	67.2	less	63.8	bottom	61.9	rich	60.3
few	67.1	wind	63.8	tall	61.9	bit	60.2
something	67.1	yet	63.8	buy	61.8	brother	60.2
thought	67.1	able	63.7	heat	61.8	clothes	60.2
large	67.0	feel	63.6	listen	61.8	note	60.2
often	67.0	rest	63.6	mark	61.8	race	60.2
show	67.0	anything	63.4	poor	61.8	hit	60.1
together	67.0	full	63.4	circle	61.7	thin	60.1
world	66.9	hold	63.4	spring	61.7	we'll	60.1
important	66.8	felt	63.3	travel	61.7	anyone	60.0
keep	66.7	hundred	63.3	hair	61.6	science	60.0
land	66.6	state	63.3	measure	61.6	break	59.9
without	66.6	stand	63.2	mountain	61.6	drive	59.9
enough	66.5	strong	63.2	nearly	61.5	pretty	59.9
life	66.5	voice	63.2	seem	61.5	corn	59.8
sometimes	66.5	piece	63.1	yourself	61.5	decide	59.8
above	66.4	river	63.1	bright	61.4	hope	59.8
almost	66.4	that's	63.1	plan	61.4	radio	59.8
country	66.1	fine	63.0	ocean	61.3	return	59.8
since	65.8	round	62.9	speed	61.3	evening	59.7
across	65.6	outside	62.7	you're	61.3	afternoon	59.6
during	65.6	power	62.7	couldn't	61.2	hole	59.6
it's	65.5	understand	62.7	middle	61.1	nose	59.6

Second Grade

quiet	59.6	season	58.1	bridge	56.6	needle	55.0
stick	59.6	we're	58.1	taste	56.6	island	54.9
teeth	59.6	mine	58.0	brave	56.5	lamp	54.9
you'll	59.6	twelve	58.0	enter	56.5	tower	54.9
cross	59.5	sadly	57.9	mostly	56.5	burn	54.8
fight	59.5	stream	57.9	park	56.5	grandfather	54.8
fill	59.5	cent	57.8	police	56.5	judge	54.8
feeling	59.4	finish	57.8	hunt	56.4	spider	54.8
meat	59.4	oxygen	57.8	lovely	56.4	stove	54.8
pass	59.4	station	57.8	tip	56.4	trick	54.8
please	59.4	tomorrow	57.8	candy	56.3	bite	54.7
west	59.4	electricity	57.7	flag	56.3	plus	54.7
kitchen	59.3	plain	57.7	gate	56.3	trunk	54.7
act	59.2	raise	57.7	jar	56.3	belt	54.6
believe	59.2	fence	57.6	wise	56.3	neighbor	54.6
safe	59.2	likely	57.6	branch	56.2	pleasure	54.6
wear	59.2	mile	57.6	fifteen	56.2	April	54.5
I'd	59.1	seat	57.6	shell	56.2	lucky	54.5
visit	59.1	bottle	57.5	pie	56.1	September	54.5
wonder	59.1	clearly	57.5	surely	56.0	pot	54.4
bank	59.0	desk	57.5	yesterday	56.0	purple	54.4
key	59.0	everywhere	57.5	basket	55.9	seed	54.4
sell	59.0	sheet	57.5	lesson	55.9	tape	54.4
sugar	59.0	smoke	57.5	sudden	55.8	racing	54.3
yard	59.0	track	57.5	thirty	55.8	canoe	54.2
fear	58.9	belong	57.4	butter	55.7	fix	54.2
rose	58.9	fifty	57.4	pink	55.7	forty	54.2
careful	58.8	giant	57.4	somewhere	55.7	fox	54.2
path	58.8	knife	57.4	gather	55.6	somehow	54.2
salt	58.8	save	57.4	leaf	55.6	welcome	54.2
chair	58.7	smell	57.4	meal	55.6	goose	54.1
dinner	58.7	deer	57.3	orange	55.6	roar	54.1
drop	58.7	ear	57.3	ranch	55.6	split	54.1
east	58.7	sweet	57.3	shirt	55.6	dirty	54.0
hurt	58.7	wave	57.3	bark	55.5	eleven	54.0
spend	58.7	bar	57.2	noon	55.5	October	54.0
count	58.6	beach	57.2	press	55.5	sink	54.0
farmer	58.6	driver	57.2	silence	55.5	pour	53.9
month	58.6	sail	57.2	teach	55.5	thumb	53.9
television	58.6	swim	57.2	wool	55.5	donkey	53.8
twice	58.6	flower	57.1	cheese	55.4	glasses	53.8
blow	58.5	handle	57.1	choice	55.4	January	53.8
dance	58.5	newspaper	57.1	dollar	55.4	shake	53.8
doctor	58.5	supper	57.1	highly	55.4	autumn	53.5
enjoy	58.5	throw	57.1	medicine	55.4	ladder	53.5
hardly	58.5	climb	57.0	anywhere	55.3	rush	53.5
quick	58.5	library	57.0	circus	55.3	tear	53.5
sister	58.5	you've	57.0	cowboy	55.3	garden	53.4
fair	58.4	earlier	56.9	lonely	55.3	juice	53.4
herself	58.4	magic	56.9	odd	55.3	nail	53.4
hungry	58.4	roof	56.9	throat	55.3	owl	53.4
loud	58.4	title	56.9	July	55.2	soup	53.4
noise	58.4	hall	56.8	June	55.2	jacket	53.3
slow	58.4	kill	56.8	pile	55.2	candle	53.2
dear	58.3	May	56.8	she's	55.2	dragon	53.2
empty	58.3	roll	56.8	tonight	55.2	float	53.2
join	58.3	vegetables	56.8	worry	55.2	flour	53.2
twenty	58.3	block	56.7	cover	55.1	November	53.2
band	58.2	lift	56.7	mirror	55.1	ugly	53.2
besides	58.2	perfect	56.7	slide	55.1	crust	53.1
fruit	58.2	shut	56.7	uncle	55.1	hammer	53.1
finger	58.1	smile	56.7	blanket	55.0	turkey	53.1
		wash	56.7	dig	55.0	everyday	53.0
		asleep	56.6	luck	55.0	lock	53.0

36

						Second Grade	
picnic	53.0	phone	50.6	weekend	47.9		
December	52.8	deliver	50.5	drain	47.7	bumpy	43.8
net	52.8	paste	50.5	jolly	47.7	doghouse	43.8
sixty	52.8	peach	50.5	nut	47.7	wall	43.8
treat	52.8	rainbow	50.5	weekly	47.6	sleigh	43.6
beef	52.7	worm	50.5	ninety	47.5	yolk	43.6
February	52.7	helicopter	50.4	robber	47.5	sausage	43.5
fold	52.7	whisper	50.4	wisely	47.5	thirteenth	43.5
thirteen	52.7	pants	50.2	blossom	47.4	chuckle	43.4
bucket	52.6	skirt	50.2	dumb	47.4	peep	43.2
chin	52.5	wander	50.2	sprinkle	47.4	kitty	43.1
joke	52.5	boil	50.1	angel	47.3	bullfrog	43.0
feather	52.4	grin	50.1	flat	47.3	pizza	43.0
hate	52.4	stare	50.1	painter	47.2	spoonful	43.0
subtract	52.4	paw	49.9	sixteenth	47.2	banker	42.9
upset	52.4	sandwich	49.9	rag	47.1	farmyard	42.7
behave	52.3	scissors	49.9	alligator	47.0	nightly	42.5
melt	52.3	homework	49.8	driveway	46.9	quack	42.5
parade	52.3	theirs	49.8	van	46.9	rightly	42.5
smart	52.3	banana	49.7	sauce	46.8	haircut	42.0
tool	52.3	brook	49.7	butcher	46.7	suppertime	41.7
fancy	52.2	seventeen	49.7	drip	46.6	ladybug	41.4
fourteen	52.2	thoughtful	49.7	eighteenth	46.6	snowman	41.4
lazy	52.1	shovel	49.6	pear	46.5	fourteenth	41.3
limit	52.1	stupid	49.6	spaceship	46.5	housework	41.3
sixteen	52.1	frighten	49.5	twig	46.5	milkman	41.1
aunt	52.0	quart	49.5	gingerbread	46.4	scratch	41.1
eagle	52.0	thirsty	49.5	bedtime	46.3	good-bye	41.0
march	52.0	whisker	49.5	chop	46.3	snowball	40.9
mix	52.0	bake	49.4	pat	46.2	beginner	40.6
ours	52.0	ballet	49.4	selfish	46.1	beehive	40.5
oven	52.0	twentieth	49.4	hood	46.0	valentine	40.2
stir	52.0	hers	49.3	pudding	46.0	pa	40.1
artist	51.9	parent	49.3	skate	46.0	bandit	40.0
fork	51.9	skating	49.3	hamburger	45.9	schoolteacher	40.0
lid	51.9	daytime	49.1	twelfth	45.8	flake	39.9
ink	51.8	crow	49.0	pup	45.7	gobble	39.9
toe	51.8	gallon	49.0	springtime	45.7	grumpy	39.9
tire	51.7	spoon	49.0	strawberry	45.7	cupid	39.6
address	51.6	tractor	48.9	tick	45.7	toaster	39.3
cheerful	51.6	farmhouse	48.8	dancer	45.6	bumblebee	39.2
glue	51.6	grocery	48.8	peel	45.6	fiftieth	39.2
chase	51.5	robin	48.8	fifteenth	45.4	August	38.8
dive	51.5	scare	48.8	salad	45.4	zipper	38.6
merry	51.5	toast	48.8	soak	45.3	noontime	38.3
parrot	51.5	rooster	48.7	thankful	45.3	grandpa	38.2
rug	51.5	seventy	48.7	trot	45.3	flatly	38.0
tooth	51.5	caterpillar	48.6	doughnut	45.2	snowflake	37.8
chance	51.4	dough	48.6	summertime	45.2	lunchtime	37.2
cheer	51.4	nineteenth	48.5	cracker	45.1	ma	37.2
blame	51.2	popcorn	48.5	jeans	45.1	pigpen	36.8
cherry	51.2	syrup	48.5	spill	45.1	teacup	36.8
downstairs	51.2	lawyer	48.4	fowl	45.0	grandma	36.7
elevator	51.2	nineteen	48.4	faraway	44.9	postcard	36.7
hut	51.2	pepper	48.4	anymore	44.7	shoestring	36.6
rub	51.2	reindeer	48.4	eleventh	44.6	bun	35.9
happiness	51.1	runner	48.4	how's	44.6	birdhouse	34.8
grandmother	51.0	bug	48.3	wintertime	44.6	paintbrush	33.7
stamp	51.0	eighty	48.3	snack	44.4	weekday	33.7
cellar	50.9	self	48.3	baker	44.3	bump	29.6
splash	50.9	carrot	48.2	gravy	44.3	sixtieth	29.6
cheek	50.8	cub	48.2	puddle	44.3	cupcake	29.0
eighteen	50.8	cereal	48.1	tadpole	44.2	bye	23.9
fairy	50.7	minus	48.1	pancake	44.1	granny	23.3
toad	50.7	greet	48.0	bless	44.0		
crazy	50.6	seventeenth	48.0	hug	43.9		
humor	50.6	chips	47.9	librarian	43.9		

use	70.9	single	61.7	board	59.8	crowd	58.2
form	66.7	correct	61.6	engine	59.8	northern	58.2
Earth	66.3	straight	61.6	method	59.8	noun	58.2
being	65.9	whose	61.6	spread	59.8	sort	58.2
study	65.9	wood	61.6	clean	59.7	army	58.1
times	65.9	moment	61.5	section	59.7	cabin	58.1
ever	65.8	square	61.5	level	59.6	California	58.1
sentence	65.6	length	61.4	silver	59.6	market	58.1
change	65.3	rather	61.4	busy	59.5	share	58.1
several	65.3	figure	61.3	coast	59.5	breath	58.0
whole	65.3	free	61.3	deal	59.5	company	58.0
against	65.1	government	61.3	sharp	59.5	danger	58.0
order	64.3	information	61.3	action	59.4	member	58.0
remember	64.2	machine	61.3	attention	59.4	neck	58.0
course	64.1	difference	61.1	cause	59.4	proper	58.0
space	64.1	famous	61.0	cool	59.4	southern	58.0
become	63.9	human	61.0	gas	59.4	valley	58.0
though	63.9	soil	61.0	type	59.4	vowel	58.0
among	63.8	iron	60.9	Africa	59.3	alive	57.9
certain	63.6	modern	60.9	alike	59.3	die	57.9
perhaps	63.6	business	60.8	scale	59.3	double	57.9
complete	63.4	case	60.8	arm	59.2	liquid	57.9
special	63.4	exactly	60.8	cost	59.2	match	57.9
list	63.3	lot	60.8	major	59.2	provide	57.9
America	63.2	reach	60.8	describe	59.1	reason	57.9
area	63.2	object	60.7	electric	59.1	till	57.9
matter	63.2	shape	60.7	office	59.1	poem	57.8
notice	63.2	village	60.7	beat	59.0	captain	57.7
surface	63.1	copy	60.6	desert	59.0	community	57.7
common	63.0	especially	60.6	inch	59.0	correctly	57.7
whether	63.0	lower	60.6	wire	59.0	discover	57.7
past	62.9	direction	60.5	cotton	58.9	dust	57.7
already	62.8	Europe	60.5	shore	58.9	everybody	57.7
either	62.8	skin	60.5	throughout	58.9	protect	57.7
instead	62.8	unit	60.5	forth	58.8	steam	57.7
meaning	62.8	difficult	60.4	metal	58.8	trail	57.7
mind	62.7	force	60.4	narrow	58.8	worth	57.7
problem	62.6	isn't	60.4	speech	58.8	baseball	57.6
system	62.5	temperature	60.4	useful	58.8	beneath	57.6
although	62.4	period	60.3	appear	58.7	range	57.6
distance	62.4	team	60.3	column	58.7	root	57.6
fact	62.4	thousand	60.3	experiment	58.7	rubber	57.6
quite	62.4	addition	60.2	knowledge	58.7	symbol	57.6
ship	62.4	amount	60.2	nation	58.7	Texas	57.6
themselves	62.4	developed	60.2	touch	58.7	win	57.6
within	62.4	born	60.1	chief	58.6	art	57.5
heart	62.3	dead	60.1	neither	58.6	chart	57.5
simple	62.3	opposite	60.1	report	58.6	flight	57.5
writing	62.3	sense	60.1	trade	58.6	nearby	57.5
main	62.2	stone	60.1	unless	58.6	plenty	57.5
pattern	62.2	there's	60.1	verb	58.6	storm	57.5
weather	62.2	wife	60.1	wheel	58.6	upper	57.5
building	62.1	cattle	60.0	church	58.5	beauty	57.4
itself	62.1	interest	60.0	familiar	58.5	flow	57.4
least	62.1	million	60.0	indeed	58.5	height	57.4
build	62.0	produce	60.0	certainly	58.4	railroad	57.4
rock	61.9	rule	60.0	final	58.4	wonderful	57.4
check	61.8	son	60.0	law	58.4	clothing	57.3
language	61.8	lead	59.9	lie	58.4	dangerous	57.3
music	61.8	sight	59.9	statement	58.4	golden	57.3
clear	61.7	thick	59.9	broke	58.3	leader	57.3
explain	61.7	Washington	59.9	tube	58.3	wheat	57.3

favorite	57.2	safety	56.2	author	55.2	**Third Grade**	
grain	57.2	strike	56.2	graph	55.2		
smooth	57.2	terrible	56.2	task	55.2	numeral	54.4
telephone	57.2	traffic	56.2	underline	55.2	pilot	54.4
continue	57.1	cell	56.1	Virginia	55.2	porch	54.4
nobody	57.1	club	56.1	we've	55.2	trace	54.4
serious	57.1	frame	56.1	burst	55.1	apartment	54.3
silent	57.1	impossible	56.1	curious	55.1	badly	54.3
western	57.1	instrument	56.1	dirt	55.1	behavior	54.3
whom	57.1	message	56.1	distant	55.1	breathe	54.3
dictionary	57.0	exact	56.0	Mississippi	55.1	creature	54.3
extra	57.0	factory	56.0	motor	55.1	handsome	54.3
scientist	57.0	fault	56.0	piano	55.1	harbor	54.3
serve	57.0	journey	56.0	respect	55.1	hay	54.3
cloud	56.9	player	56.0	silk	55.1	insect	54.3
enemy	56.9	rhythm	56.0	swing	55.1	mainly	54.3
fellow	56.9	Alaska	55.9	anyway	55.0	nails	54.3
manner	56.9	deck	55.9	highway	55.0	package	54.3
remain	56.9	dozen	55.9	offer	55.0	pale	54.3
student	56.9	football	55.9	pain	55.0	writer	54.3
suit	56.9	pipe	55.9	tea	55.0	bend	54.2
they're	56.9	rod	55.9	upward	55.0	eager	54.2
tongue	56.9	ruler	55.9	brush	54.9	flame	54.2
charge	56.8	allow	55.8	comfortable	54.9	guard	54.2
daughter	56.8	bent	55.8	orbit	54.9	officer	54.2
direct	56.8	bill	55.8	president	54.9	saddle	54.2
education	56.8	Chicago	55.8	tent	54.9	settle	54.2
growth	56.8	daily	55.8	waste	54.9	wound	54.2
he'd	56.8	fuel	55.8	accident	54.8	adventure	54.1
lose	56.8	haven't	55.8	bicycle	54.8	birth	54.1
pleasant	56.8	pole	55.8	buffalo	54.8	command	54.1
swimming	56.8	replace	55.8	castle	54.8	crack	54.1
agree	56.7	you'd	55.8	crop	54.8	difficulty	54.1
bow	56.7	chest	55.7	gasoline	54.8	ill	54.1
clip	56.7	courage	55.7	transportation	54.8	Ohio	54.1
copper	56.7	rice	55.7	worse	54.8	rear	54.1
design	56.7	shade	55.7	arrange	54.7	weren't	54.1
equipment	56.7	thread	55.7	earn	54.7	aboard	54.0
secret	56.7	discovery	55.6	explore	54.7	dull	54.0
skill	56.7	honor	55.6	hollow	54.7	firm	54.0
sunlight	56.7	load	55.6	stairs	54.7	hospital	54.0
brain	56.6	ought	55.6	alphabet	54.6	jungle	54.0
planet	56.6	queen	55.6	Australia	54.6	plastic	54.0
Asia	56.5	shadow	55.6	aware	54.6	shelf	54.0
clay	56.5	tight	55.6	he'll	54.6	voyage	54.0
escape	56.5	tin	55.6	remove	54.6	arrive	53.9
prove	56.5	bare	55.5	select	54.6	bet	53.9
attack	56.4	classroom	55.5	stomach	54.6	camera	53.9
search	56.4	leather	55.5	weigh	54.6	fierce	53.9
sir	56.4	pack	55.5	anybody	54.5	label	53.9
weak	56.4	straw	55.5	consonant	54.5	opinion	53.9
bone	56.3	strip	55.5	false	54.5	pasture	53.9
cream	56.3	husband	55.4	grade	54.5	sale	53.9
excitement	56.3	pound	55.4	mistake	54.5	shelter	53.9
log	56.3	prepare	55.4	owner	54.5	shine	53.9
o'clock	56.3	pure	55.4	passage	54.5	slave	53.9
outer	56.3	shoot	55.4	screen	54.5	soldier	53.9
sick	56.3	substance	55.4	somebody	54.5	whistle	53.9
article	56.2	worn	55.4	stranger	54.5	arithmetic	53.8
automobile	56.2	fog	55.3	tribe	54.5	calm	53.8
court	56.2	globe	55.3	curve	54.4	garage	53.8
darkness	56.2	pine	55.3	Florida	54.4	neighborhood	53.8
eastern	56.2	triangle	55.3	gift	54.4	palace	53.8
pond	56.2	arrow	55.2	magnet	54.4	selection	53.8

Third Grade

Word	Score	Word	Score	Word	Score	Word	Score
warning	53.8	Massachusetts	52.8	switch	52.2	shy	51.5
adult	53.7	palm	52.8	they'd	52.2	tender	51.5
coach	53.7	someday	52.8	tunnel	52.2	bother	51.4
deeply	53.7	stuff	52.8	upstairs	52.2	cone	51.4
Illinois	53.7	thermometer	52.8	weary	52.2	crown	51.4
stiff	53.7	truly	52.8	loop	52.1	dock	51.4
tune	53.7	worker	52.8	pioneer	52.1	hunger	51.4
breeze	53.6	addend	52.7	prince	52.1	Michigan	51.4
Pennsylvania	53.6	airport	52.7	ticket	52.1	wisdom	51.4
shed	53.6	coin	52.7	underwater	52.1	coral	51.3
brick	53.5	damp	52.7	attitude	52.0	dare	51.3
contest	53.5	pitcher	52.7	bunch	52.0	frost	51.3
desire	53.5	quarter	52.7	Colorado	52.0	index	51.3
habit	53.5	statue	52.7	colt	52.0	knock	51.3
mill	53.5	they'll	52.7	creek	52.0	pupil	51.3
ourselves	53.5	wake	52.7	meadow	52.0	shouldn't	51.3
rhyme	53.5	bench	52.6	noisy	52.0	beard	51.2
soap	53.5	clue	52.6	rid	52.0	borrow	51.2
vacation	53.5	flash	52.6	witch	52.0	curtain	51.2
female	53.4	flush	52.6	beaver	51.9	guest	51.2
foolish	53.4	hook	52.6	cliff	51.9	hatch	51.2
ghost	53.4	sidewalk	52.6	department	51.9	Oregon	51.2
stem	53.4	treasure	52.6	gathering	51.9	battery	51.1
sunshine	53.4	altogether	52.5	mold	51.9	costume	51.1
awake	53.3	bitter	52.5	nickel	51.9	delicious	51.1
backward	53.3	doorway	52.5	queer	51.9	flashlight	51.1
cardboard	53.3	entrance	52.5	reply	51.9	goodness	51.1
chocolate	53.3	grand	52.5	spare	51.9	lump	51.1
clever	53.3	mild	52.5	sword	51.9	rat	51.1
code	53.3	neat	52.5	tap	51.9	restaurant	51.1
herd	53.3	visitor	52.5	bible	51.8	sweep	51.1
potato	53.3	colorful	52.4	craft	51.8	alongside	51.0
laughter	53.2	fool	52.4	cruel	51.8	boss	51.0
lightning	53.2	forever	52.4	dinosaur	51.8	dim	51.0
Missouri	53.2	princess	52.4	governor	51.8	knot	51.0
beam	53.1	pump	52.4	Kansas	51.8	steal	51.0
blend	53.1	rainfall	52.4	kick	51.8	clover	50.9
ceiling	53.1	relief	52.4	mention	51.8	disappear	50.9
drum	53.1	ripe	52.4	moonlight	51.8	excuse	50.9
lawn	53.1	sample	52.4	shock	51.8	gum	50.9
male	53.1	shortly	52.4	whip	51.8	hem	50.9
overhead	53.1	stable	52.4	bath	51.7	moss	50.9
sunny	53.1	underground	52.4	Hawaii	51.7	mule	50.9
decision	53.0	beast	52.3	punctuation	51.7	pail	50.9
faint	53.0	diamond	52.3	tale	51.7	pronoun	50.9
hey	53.0	feast	52.3	anxious	51.6	repair	50.9
magazine	53.0	Jackson	52.3	bundle	51.6	Tennessee	50.9
marry	53.0	lap	52.3	collar	51.6	waist	50.9
pretend	53.0	monster	52.3	dime	51.6	apron	50.8
religion	53.0	remind	52.3	drag	51.6	broom	50.8
shiny	53.0	thunder	52.3	invite	51.6	canyon	50.8
underneath	53.0	trust	52.3	Kentucky	51.6	container	50.8
content	52.9	aim	52.2	knee	51.6	county	50.8
delight	52.9	alarm	52.2	mayor	51.6	fearful	50.8
oak	52.9	harvest	52.2	muddy	51.6	helmet	50.8
settlement	52.9	hotel	52.2	museum	51.6	Maine	50.8
basketball	52.8	lean	52.2	nurse	51.6	shepherd	50.8
bedroom	52.8	microscope	52.2	pronounce	51.6	spacecraft	50.8
comfort	52.8	mystery	52.2	sack	51.6	spark	50.8
harm	52.8	patch	52.2	anger	51.5	Arizona	50.7
item	52.8	puzzle	52.2	awful	51.5	bacon	50.7
lad	52.8	rider	52.2	meter	51.5	chimney	50.7
		she'd	52.2	notebook	51.5	Georgia	50.7
		soda	52.2	playground	51.5	nowhere	50.7

plow	50.7	margin	49.7	heap	48.8		
terror	50.7	crocodile	49.6	hell	48.8		
twist	50.7	cube	49.6	kingdom	48.8	protest	48.1
Connecticut	50.6	fiction	49.6	moth	48.8	sew	48.1
drift	50.6	helpless	49.6	necklace	48.8	sleeve	48.1
northwest	50.6	hum	49.6	ox	48.8	attic	48.0
pillow	50.6	Louisiana	49.6	sigh	48.8	belly	48.0
remainder	50.6	mist	49.6	chew	48.7	cornfield	48.0
rent	50.6	prayer	49.6	plainly	48.7	foil	48.0
dash	50.5	reporter	49.6	prisoner	48.7	gloves	48.0
greeting	50.5	she'll	49.6	scarf	48.7	hoop	48.0
refrigerator	50.5	skunk	49.6	Alabama	48.6	juicy	48.0
rewrite	50.5	southwest	49.6	apostrophe	48.6	oval	48.0
thief	50.5	spray	49.6	argue	48.6	pistil	48.0
wrap	50.5	warn	49.6	awhile	48.6	bathroom	47.9
wreck	50.5	refuse	49.5	bounce	48.6	beetle	47.9
crawl	50.4	tag	49.5	burro	48.6	catcher	47.9
evil	50.4	violin	49.5	curiously	48.6	drawer	47.9
fist	50.4	bubble	49.4	friendship	48.6	lemonade	47.9
grab	50.4	carpet	49.4	lone	48.6	Minnesota	47.9
grown-up	50.4	lane	49.4	Nevada	48.6	relax	47.9
hose	50.4	pray	49.4	praise	48.6	seize	47.9
inn	50.4	purse	49.4	schedule	48.6	starfish	47.9
northeast	50.4	roast	49.4	umbrella	48.6	wildlife	47.9
examine	50.3	sheriff	49.4	willow	48.6	woolen	47.9
guitar	50.3	southeast	49.4	backwards	48.5	balcony	47.8
steer	50.3	stew	49.4	Indiana	48.5	caution	47.8
swallow	50.3	chalkboard	49.3	Iowa	48.5	clam	47.8
thickness	50.3	seashore	49.3	Maryland	48.5	devil	47.8
twin	50.3	tan	49.3	miserable	48.5	hound	47.8
handkerchief	50.2	carpenter	49.2	Nebraska	48.5	kit	47.8
olive	50.2	elbow	49.2	orchard	48.5	pigeon	47.8
polite	50.2	obey	49.2	roam	48.5	strap	47.8
tub	50.2	professor	49.2	ruin	48.5	beg	47.7
alert	50.1	reward	49.2	Utah	48.5	buggy	47.7
careless	50.1	skip	49.2	Wisconsin	48.5	cricket	47.7
comb	50.1	slippery	49.2	actor	48.4	downhill	47.7
detective	50.1	stool	49.2	drug	48.4	lettuce	47.7
fountain	50.1	strangely	49.2	Oklahoma	48.4	lighthouse	47.7
garbage	50.1	sunrise	49.2	puff	48.4	luckily	47.7
rectangle	50.1	unpleasant	49.2	sap	48.4	outdoors	47.7
satisfy	50.1	velvet	49.2	scrape	48.4	pajamas	47.7
snap	50.1	assignment	49.1	stack	48.4	pedal	47.7
wrist	50.1	dairy	49.1	Antarctica	48.3	puppet	47.7
kindness	50.0	enjoyment	49.1	bury	48.3	stillness	47.7
nonsense	50.0	lace	49.1	campfire	48.3	ton	47.7
paddle	50.0	mask	49.1	lizard	48.3	chatter	47.6
wicked	50.0	sweater	49.1	lookout	48.3	fireworks	47.6
winner	50.0	cab	49.0	Montana	48.3	frown	47.6
crab	49.9	Houston	49.0	plug	48.3	schoolhouse	47.6
downtown	49.9	chalk	48.9	they've	48.3	foggy	47.5
encyclopedia	49.9	corral	48.9	comma	48.2	fry	47.5
loaf	49.9	handwriting	48.9	goldfish	48.2	modest	47.5
mosquito	49.9	jail	48.9	hillside	48.2	alley	47.4
pollen	49.9	maid	48.9	hive	48.2	hire	47.4
spoil	49.9	peas	48.9	kangaroo	48.2	subtraction	47.4
computer	49.8	pirate	48.9	lip	48.2	taxi	47.4
Delaware	49.8	robot	48.9	signature	48.2	creep	47.3
freeze	49.8	saucer	48.9	spy	48.2	mat	47.3
okay	49.8	squeeze	48.9	Arkansas	48.1	rude	47.3
pumpkin	49.8	towel	48.9	beak	48.1	wink	47.3
tray	49.8	Wyoming	48.9	fossil	48.1	announce	47.2
yarn	49.8	customer	48.8	hawk	48.1	blackboard	47.2
indoors	49.7	drugstore	48.8	kiss	48.1	denominator	47.2

Third Grade

firewood	47.2	hopefully	46.3	onion	45.2	grapefruit	43.9
hips	47.2	housewife	46.3	pane	45.2	rip	43.8
lemon	47.2	motel	46.3	tighten	45.2	stair	43.8
nickname	47.2	railing	46.3	yeast	45.2	barnyard	43.7
schoolroom	47.2	starve	46.3	boxing	45.1	bead	43.7
singer	47.2	bathtub	46.2	jerk	45.1	churn	43.7
crooked	47.1	celery	46.2	Vermont	45.1	fudge	43.7
elementary	47.1	cozy	46.2	boxer	45.0	grape	43.7
gaze	47.1	crank	46.2	gull	45.0	overflow	43.7
jeep	47.1	Denver	46.2	teaspoon	45.0	woodpecker	43.7
robe	47.1	leak	46.2	tremble	45.0	bracelet	43.6
roller	47.1	Miami	46.2	approve	44.9	mush	43.6
sadness	47.1	tomato	46.2	cape	44.9	purr	43.6
scrub	47.1	watermelon	46.2	holder	44.9	berry	43.5
trailer	47.1	drown	46.1	poster	44.8	booklet	43.5
complain	47.0	reptile	46.1	teapot	44.8	cartoon	43.5
crisp	47.0	cocoon	46.0	trash	44.8	harp	43.5
dislike	47.0	flee	46.0	chunk	44.7	oatmeal	43.5
duckling	47.0	glide	46.0	crash	44.7	shrink	43.5
giraffe	47.0	rib	46.0	drowsy	44.7	straighten	43.5
heel	47.0	skyscraper	46.0	fir	44.7	dwarf	43.4
pint	47.0	supermarket	46.0	flutter	44.7	homesick	43.4
rake	47.0	cute	45.9	germ	44.7	lasso	43.4
windmill	47.0	digit	45.9	sip	44.7	nimble	43.4
beggar	46.9	moan	45.9	slipper	44.7	motorcycle	43.3
squeak	46.9	scatter	45.9	wheelbarrow	44.7	numerator	43.3
unlikely	46.9	tease	45.9	ache	44.6	shorts	43.3
weep	46.9	ad	45.8	chipmunk	44.6	adopt	43.2
wipe	46.9	carve	45.8	curl	44.6	grandchildren	43.2
caribou	46.8	dandelion	45.8	disturb	44.6	rob	43.2
entertain	46.8	exit	45.8	gardener	44.6	sweets	43.2
movable	46.8	gown	45.8	snowstorm	44.6	tickle	43.2
rodeo	46.8	greasy	45.8	teakettle	44.6	ambulance	43.1
sneeze	46.8	loosen	45.8	Dallas	44.5	cemetery	43.1
thirst	46.8	scrapbook	45.8	doorstep	44.5	snowfall	43.1
tug	46.8	shrimp	45.8	joyous	44.5	whoop	43.1
advice	46.7	waiter	45.8	unfair	44.5	foolishly	43.0
cleaner	46.7	pal	45.7	unkind	44.5	poppy	43.0
dump	46.7	sill	45.7	tulip	44.4	schoolyard	43.0
limb	46.7	sour	45.7	vest	44.4	sparkle	43.0
dessert	46.6	builder	45.6	zebra	44.4	trainer	43.0
doorbell	46.6	fulcrum	45.6	elm	44.3	bunk	42.9
lick	46.6	scar	45.6	hurrah	44.3	mumps	42.9
mushroom	46.6	shorten	45.6	sniff	44.3	overcoat	42.9
shiver	46.6	unfriendly	45.6	clubhouse	44.2	schoolboy	42.9
slap	46.6	waterfall	45.6	recite	44.2	ass	42.8
stocking	46.6	blessing	45.5	riverbank	44.2	beware	42.8
vacant	46.6	eraser	45.5	boast	44.1	chimpanzee	42.7
buzz	46.5	kindergarten	45.5	fern	44.1	kennel	42.7
furry	46.5	mammal	45.5	scold	44.1	poplar	42.7
leopard	46.5	perimeter	45.5	uphill	44.1	radish	42.7
playful	46.5	wow	45.5	buckle	44.0	raspberry	42.7
tasty	46.5	claw	45.4	gasp	44.0	untie	42.7
bakery	46.4	growl	45.4	headline	44.0	blink	42.6
dread	46.4	nod	45.4	mountaintop	44.0	deerskin	42.6
elastic	46.4	swish	45.4	mow	44.0	errand	42.6
howl	46.4	unload	45.4	raincoat	44.0	exclaim	42.6
Idaho	46.4	clap	45.3	satin	44.0	larva	42.6
killer	46.4	horseshoe	45.3	soar	44.0	pathway	42.6
punish	46.4	husky	45.3	watchful	44.0	squeal	42.6
bald	46.3	scarecrow	45.3	wiggle	44.0	yawn	42.6
helium	46.3	amuse	45.2	braid	43.9	actress	42.5
		greedy	45.2	capitalize	43.9	avenue	42.5
		joyful	45.2	chick	43.9	flagpole	42.5

grocer	42.5	hometown	40.7	shopper	38.4
shove	42.5	indoor	40.7	sunglasses	38.3
yardstick	42.5	wed	40.7	bathrobe	38.2
erase	42.4	doorknob	40.5	granddaughter	38.2
mop	42.4	raindrop	40.5	sundae	38.2
shave	42.4	raisin	40.5	whoosh	38.2
swirl	42.4	wastebasket	40.5	tinfoil	38.1
touchdown	42.4	wig	40.5	grandson	38.0
unhappily	42.4	ape	40.4	spaceman	38.0
sob	42.3	cheat	40.4	houseboat	37.8
tortoise	42.3	bloom	40.3	workroom	37.8
airmail	42.2	germinate	40.3	cupful	37.7
bonnet	42.2	cranberry	40.2	fairyland	37.7
nephew	42.2	fingertip	40.2	motorboat	37.7
thousandth	42.1	niece	40.2	marshal	37.6
badge	42.0	petal	40.2	taxicab	37.6
elves	42.0	cleverly	40.1	carol	37.5
hibernate	42.0	dent	40.1	necktie	37.5
workman	42.0	falcon	40.1	snowdrift	37.5
gulp	41.9	hourly	40.1	fife	37.4
shoemaker	41.9	loser	40.1	mutter	37.4
jingle	41.8	daisy	40.0	cucumber	37.3
shellfish	41.8	troll	40.0	eggshell	37.3
speedy	41.8	caw	39.9	honeybee	37.3
unfold	41.8	jigsaw	39.9	quicksand	37.3
bud	41.7	lifeboat	39.9	bib	37.2
eyeglasses	41.7	barbecue	39.8	exam	37.2
faucet	41.7	blackberry	39.8	meow	37.2
pest	41.7	mailbox	39.8	lifeguard	37.1
sunburn	41.7	sin	39.8	playpen	37.1
whimper	41.7	bearskin	39.7	ringmaster	37.1
annoy	41.6	folder	39.7	unscrew	37.1
bleed	41.6	peek	39.7	cob	37.0
heater	41.6	ripple	39.7	fake	37.0
rename	41.6	unpack	39.7	snowplow	37.0
slumber	41.6	earring	39.6	beater	36.9
unlock	41.6	elf	39.6	rink	36.9
margarine	41.5	lollipop	39.6	celebrate	36.8
ripen	41.5	mulberry	39.6	hamster	36.8
rosebush	41.5	nightgown	39.6	lunchroom	36.8
snort	41.5	eardrum	39.5	whir	36.8
autograph	41.4	sealskin	39.5	daffodil	36.7
burglar	41.4	excite	39.4	dishwasher	36.7
giggle	41.4	flop	39.4	firecracker	36.7
upside-down	41.4	goatskin	39.4	washcloth	36.6
dodge	41.3	zip	39.4	clop	36.5
bulldozer	41.2	campsite	39.3	hopscotch	36.4
fencing	41.2	stripe	39.3	buttonhole	36.3
pageant	41.2	midget	39.2	bum	36.2
watchdog	41.2	baboon	39.1	holster	36.2
partridge	41.1	gorilla	39.1	slowdown	36.2
quiz	41.1	rainwater	39.1	babe	36.1
fingernail	41.0	zoom	39.1	storybook	36.1
album	40.9	blueberry	38.9	wriggle	36.1
caveman	40.9	cluck	38.9	marshmallow	36.0
forgive	40.9	slime	38.8	cowhand	35.9
lilac	40.9	someplace	38.8	pilgrim	35.9
lullaby	40.9	headband	38.7	pillowcase	35.9
squawk	40.9	housekeeping	38.7	sprinkler	35.9
chili	40.8	pus	38.7	hydrant	35.8
disobey	40.8	teaspoonful	38.7	slowpoke	35.8
horsehair	40.8	blot	38.5	horsehide	35.6
storeroom	40.8	earthworm	38.4	cobble	35.5
apology	40.7	mousetrap	38.4	ukulele	35.5

Third Grade

graham	35.2
shipbuilder	35.2
cattail	35.1
check-up	35.1
liter	35.1
dreamland	35.0
manhole	35.0
toboggan	35.0
bicycling	34.8
parka	34.8
setback	34.8
rooftop	34.7
forgiveness	34.5
pant	34.5
cheep	34.4
spank	34.3
fingerprint	34.0
playhouse	34.0
shoelace	34.0
unroll	34.0
icicle	33.9
wrongly	33.9
mall	33.8
escalator	33.7
honk	33.6
homemaker	33.5
waffle	32.9
uncover	32.8
brownie	32.3
popgun	32.3
windup	32.2
front-page	32.1
tiptoe	31.9
pooh	31.7
trickle	31.7
seagull	31.4
baptism	31.3
grandparent	31.3
waitress	31.3
foursquare	31.0
fib	30.6
war	30.6
blast-off	30.5
snob	30.3
splatter	30.2
stamen	29.9
bedspring	29.6
hangar	29.6
milkmaid	29.6
unfasten	29.2
diaper	29.0
cutout	27.7
millionth	27.7
handbag	25.9
treetop	25.5
ting	22.1

however	65.6	related	57.9	hadn't	56.2	youth	54.9
example	65.3	coal	57.8	hide	56.2	becoming	54.8
base	61.6	experience	57.8	recognize	56.2	locate	54.8
thus	61.5	future	57.8	sum	56.2	topic	54.8
present	61.4	Mexico	57.8	appearance	56.1	active	54.7
except	61.3	stage	57.8	aren't	56.1	machinery	54.7
suppose	61.3	compound	57.7	Canada	56.1	steep	54.7
history	61.1	further	57.7	character	56.1	tough	54.7
necessary	60.6	guide	57.7	diagram	56.1	unlike	54.7
subject	60.5	scientific	57.7	setting	56.1	adjective	54.6
wasn't	60.5	usual	57.7	somewhat	56.1	Columbus	54.6
general	60.4	industry	57.6	Spain	56.1	enormous	54.6
material	60.4	popular	57.6	steady	56.1	event	54.6
blood	60.3	support	57.6	avoid	56.0	loss	54.6
region	60.3	development	57.5	doubt	56.0	plural	54.6
doesn't	60.2	master	57.5	situation	56.0	raw	54.6
result	60.2	observe	57.4	effort	55.9	salmon	54.6
various	60.2	structure	57.4	carbon	55.8	tank	54.6
control	59.8	tone	57.4	foreign	55.8	accept	54.5
France	59.8	whatever	57.4	greatly	55.8	blind	54.5
position	59.8	chapter	57.3	Japan	55.8	compass	54.5
similar	59.8	immediately	57.3	continent	55.7	mood	54.5
wouldn't	59.7	peace	57.3	occur	55.7	poet	54.5
ancient	59.6	Italy	57.2	blank	55.6	seldom	54.5
century	59.6	powerful	57.2	native	55.6	thou	54.5
death	59.6	score	57.2	prevent	55.6	universe	54.5
therefore	59.6	service	57.2	suggest	55.6	colony	54.4
beyond	59.5	atmosphere	57.1	truth	55.6	definition	54.4
actually	59.3	broad	57.1	college	55.5	perfectly	54.4
basic	59.3	climate	57.1	date	55.5	struggle	54.4
contain	59.1	coffee	57.1	factor	55.5	vote	54.4
equal	59.0	Germany	57.1	furniture	55.5	activity	54.3
total	59.0	model	57.1	depend	55.4	halfway	54.3
value	59.0	view	57.1	partly	55.4	happening	54.3
exercise	58.9	whenever	57.1	audience	55.3	Mars	54.3
movement	58.9	ordinary	57.0	collection	55.3	syllable	54.3
nature	58.8	program	57.0	condition	55.3	actual	54.2
public	58.8	rough	57.0	conversation	55.3	atom	54.2
simply	58.8	series	57.0	receive	55.3	engineer	54.2
steel	58.8	chemical	56.9	aid	55.2	organization	54.2
separate	58.7	freedom	56.9	construction	55.2	port	54.2
paragraph	58.6	individual	56.8	improve	55.2	tropical	54.2
particular	58.6	national	56.8	principal	55.2	invention	54.1
pressure	58.6	battle	56.6	research	55.2	mental	54.1
solve	58.6	health	56.6	couple	55.1	movie	54.1
what's	58.6	particularly	56.6	create	55.1	private	54.1
original	58.5	property	56.6	degree	55.1	tide	54.1
rise	58.4	scene	56.6	realize	55.1	brass	54.0
effect	58.3	discuss	56.5	route	55.1	definite	54.0
motion	58.3	division	56.5	thee	55.1	equally	54.0
supply	58.3	shoulders	56.5	aside	55.0	location	54.0
entire	58.2	social	56.5	collect	55.0	mixture	54.0
solid	58.2	valuable	56.5	combination	55.0	brief	53.9
expect	58.1	ability	56.4	excellent	55.0	cast	53.9
regular	58.1	balance	56.4	lack	55.0	dawn	53.9
represent	58.1	bat	56.4	repeat	55.0	film	53.9
current	58.0	crew	56.4	unknown	55.0	fort	53.9
express	58.0	increase	56.4	brisk	54.9	fully	53.9
phrase	58.0	success	56.4	religious	54.9	gravity	53.9
purpose	58.0	successful	56.3	stretch	54.9	labor	53.9
strength	58.0	volume	56.3	wherever	54.9	thy	53.9
average	57.9	central	56.2	willing	54.9	divide	53.8

							Fourth Grade	
memory	53.8	bulb	52.9	cousin	52.1			
pride	53.8	commercial	52.9	cylinder	52.1			
slip	53.8	gentleman	52.9	Venus	52.1	lifetime	51.3
vapor	53.8	practically	52.9	attract	52.0	manage	51.3
damage	53.7	approach	52.8	ease	52.0	manager	51.3
depth	53.7	arrangement	52.8	expert	52.0	pad	51.3
exchange	53.7	bay	52.8	maintain	52.0	proof	51.3
exist	53.7	carriage	52.8	raft	52.0	slice	51.3
hunter	53.7	committee	52.8	wedding	52.0	telegraph	51.3
image	53.7	construct	52.8	afford	51.9	anchor	51.2
poetry	53.7	favor	52.8	capture	51.9	cement	51.2
precious	53.7	here's	52.8	cash	51.9	confidence	51.2
remarkable	53.7	measurement	52.8	forehead	51.9	crystal	51.2
shallow	53.7	prefer	52.8	fortune	51.9	fame	51.2
border	53.6	primary	52.8	glow	51.9	fortunately	51.2
instant	53.6	attend	52.7	pronunciation	51.9	maple	51.2
mathematics	53.6	billion	52.7	vocabulary	51.9	sensitive	51.2
mission	53.6	destroy	52.7	volcano	51.9	champion	51.1
mysterious	53.6	minor	52.7	household	51.8	cottage	51.1
Philadelphia	53.6	muscle	52.7	operate	51.8	ray	51.1
practical	53.6	seek	52.7	parenthesis	51.8	reduce	51.1
wealth	53.6	width	52.7	hasn't	51.7	agriculture	51.0
estimate	53.5	civilization	52.6	horseback	51.7	ax	51.0
fireplace	53.5	consider	52.6	lens	51.7	bull	51.0
goal	53.5	cord	52.6	manufacture	51.7	harmful	51.0
heading	53.5	daylight	52.6	pause	51.7	multiplication	51.0
possibly	53.5	passenger	52.6	tole	51.7	nitrogen	51.0
slight	53.5	patient	52.6	union	51.7	skillful	51.0
solar	53.5	peaceful	52.6	annual	51.6	suffix	51.0
background	53.4	rapid	52.6	argument	51.6	blast	50.9
glance	53.4	uniform	52.6	assembly	51.6	convenient	50.9
imagination	53.4	warmth	52.6	capable	51.6	curiosity	50.9
lively	53.4	acid	52.5	colonial	51.6	liberty	50.9
meanwhile	53.4	challenge	52.5	dioxide	51.6	permit	50.9
telescope	53.4	drill	52.5	fasten	51.6	policy	50.9
expensive	53.3	moist	52.5	flesh	51.6	ridge	50.9
fraction	53.3	cane	52.4	Jupiter	51.6	sunset	50.9
hydrogen	53.3	career	52.4	lever	51.6	blade	50.8
lumber	53.3	navy	52.4	slender	51.6	define	50.8
prairie	53.3	stroke	52.4	useless	51.6	dense	50.8
responsible	53.3	holiday	52.3	bold	51.5	echo	50.8
fashion	53.2	legend	52.3	decimal	51.5	file	50.8
midnight	53.2	multiply	52.3	establish	51.5	gear	50.8
performance	53.2	orchestra	52.3	fail	51.5	Holland	50.8
culture	53.1	predicate	52.3	gentlemen	51.5	kid	50.8
flood	53.1	revolution	52.3	geography	51.5	lava	50.8
laboratory	53.1	royal	52.3	horizontal	51.5	regard	50.8
moisture	53.1	singular	52.3	icy	51.5	rescue	50.8
relative	53.1	sweat	52.3	kettle	51.5	heaven	50.7
rifle	53.1	web	52.3	medium	51.5	introduction	50.7
sport	53.1	aluminum	52.2	peak	51.5	invent	50.7
staff	53.1	citizen	52.2	possession	51.5	artificial	50.6
territory	53.1	clearing	52.2	prison	51.5	connection	50.6
wilderness	53.1	custom	52.2	spear	51.5	drama	50.6
altitude	53.0	cycle	52.2	communicate	51.4	earthquake	50.6
cabbage	53.0	downward	52.2	confusion	51.4	intelligent	50.6
dam	53.0	electronic	52.2	diet	51.4	magnificent	50.6
electrical	53.0	leap	52.2	furnace	51.4	poison	50.6
folk	53.0	partner	52.2	hind	51.4	polar	50.6
platform	53.0	sphere	52.2	rail	51.4	upright	50.6
satellite	53.0	tend	52.2	wax	51.4	closet	50.5
submarine	53.0	circular	52.1	agreement	51.3	empire	50.5
swift	53.0	council	52.1	error	51.3	hobby	50.5
accent	52.9	counter	52.1	honest	51.3	intelligence	50.5

Fourth Grade

Word		Word		Word		Word	
lantern	50.5	envelope	49.8	basin	49.2	gap	48.6
recording	50.5	grateful	49.8	brand	49.2	patrol	48.6
shrill	50.5	scent	49.8	courtyard	49.2	prism	48.6
flock	50.4	temple	49.8	creative	49.2	secretary	48.6
handful	50.4	admit	49.7	fetch	49.2	absorb	48.5
organ	50.4	calendar	49.7	limestone	49.2	affair	48.5
rage	50.4	celebration	49.7	messenger	49.2	appreciate	48.5
stall	50.4	chord	49.7	outfit	49.2	athletic	48.5
zone	50.4	ditch	49.7	partial	49.2	crime	48.5
awkward	50.3	grease	49.7	Pittsburgh	49.2	exhibit	48.5
consist	50.3	haul	49.7	routine	49.2	flavor	48.5
defend	50.3	ideal	49.7	rural	49.2	glorious	48.5
dependent	50.3	patience	49.7	scenery	49.2	graze	48.5
dew	50.3	protective	49.7	scout	49.2	junior	48.5
director	50.3	pyramid	49.7	steak	49.2	sideways	48.5
elsewhere	50.3	sensible	49.7	streak	49.2	thump	48.5
examination	50.3	tame	49.7	widow	49.2	adjust	48.4
jewelry	50.3	trim	49.7	clumsy	49.1	grace	48.4
oats	50.3	worship	49.7	diary	49.1	hail	48.4
organize	50.3	admire	49.6	guy	49.1	humorous	48.4
prefix	50.3	belief	49.6	headquarters	49.1	lime	48.4
rectangular	50.3	bullet	49.6	instruction	49.1	savings	48.4
restless	50.3	capsule	49.6	marble	49.1	strict	48.4
shift	50.3	cluster	49.6	prehistoric	49.1	triangular	48.4
slant	50.3	deadly	49.6	approximate	49.0	typewriter	48.4
boundary	50.2	desperate	49.6	breast	49.0	cable	48.3
childhood	50.2	diver	49.6	bride	49.0	dentist	48.3
coastal	50.2	festival	49.6	convince	49.0	grip	48.3
editor	50.2	hint	49.6	faith	49.0	imitate	48.3
fisherman	50.2	irrigation	49.6	golf	49.0	lunar	48.3
melody	50.2	ledge	49.6	hush	49.0	salesman	48.3
vibrate	50.2	nucleus	49.6	pity	49.0	snail	48.3
channel	50.1	overnight	49.6	vegetation	49.0	weed	48.3
contrary	50.1	servant	49.6	volcanic	49.0	carrier	48.2
gang	50.1	suffer	49.6	cork	48.9	definitely	48.2
occupation	50.1	terribly	49.6	deaf	48.9	disappointment	48.2
pit	50.1	text	49.6	den	48.9	fluid	48.2
sake	50.1	trousers	49.6	hastily	48.9	grammar	48.2
stalk	50.1	bomb	49.5	inventor	48.9	innocent	48.2
balanced	50.0	carton	49.5	naked	48.9	mast	48.2
bamboo	50.0	charm	49.5	screw	48.9	mount	48.2
brake	50.0	contraction	49.5	squash	48.9	rattle	48.2
core	50.0	generous	49.5	succeed	48.9	riddle	48.2
enthusiasm	50.0	lord	49.5	swell	48.9	Seattle	48.2
harsh	50.0	perfume	49.5	absence	48.8	fade	48.1
immediate	50.0	skim	49.5	assistant	48.8	grind	48.1
introduce	50.0	sponge	49.5	cure	48.8	jaw	48.1
novel	50.0	superior	49.5	dreadful	48.8	nylon	48.1
quit	50.0	where's	49.5	fortunate	48.8	railway	48.1
Saturn	50.0	barrel	49.4	rigid	48.8	rely	48.1
chorus	49.9	Fahrenheit	49.4	tackle	48.8	talent	48.1
friction	49.9	framework	49.4	unfamiliar	48.8	charcoal	48.0
objective	49.9	mane	49.4	calves	48.7	comment	48.0
pottery	49.9	occasional	49.4	continental	48.7	dial	48.0
raccoon	49.9	sturdy	49.4	liver	48.7	grasshopper	48.0
swamp	49.9	vehicle	49.4	mantle	48.7	holy	48.0
aquarium	49.8	batter	49.3	plaster	48.7	jug	48.0
bronze	49.8	emergency	49.3	remark	48.7	livestock	48.0
cheap	49.8	explorer	49.3	stole	48.7	pistol	48.0
coarse	49.8	glimpse	49.3	uncomfortable	48.7	Pluto	48.0
concert	49.8	operator	49.3	bargain	48.6	polish	48.0
dip	49.8	quarrel	49.3	chill	48.6	sore	48.0
		respond	49.3	costly	48.6	trader	48.0
		shame	49.3	electron	48.6	cocoa	47.9

comic	47.9	beloved	47.3	parcel	46.7	**Fourth Grade**	
disaster	47.9	concentrate	47.3	scalp	46.7		
humble	47.9	deposit	47.3	textbook	46.7	whirl	46.1
lately	47.9	gypsy	47.3	Uranus	46.7	blouse	46.0
nursery	47.9	insist	47.3	vase	46.7	buyer	46.0
ounce	47.9	kernel	47.3	vine	46.7	fin	46.0
photo	47.9	propeller	47.3	arctic	46.6	flea	46.0
seaweed	47.9	ridiculous	47.3	breathless	46.6	metric	46.0
solo	47.9	stubborn	47.3	essay	46.6	myth	46.0
troublesome	47.9	stump	47.3	hopeless	46.6	pardon	46.0
whoever	47.9	wharf	47.3	mend	46.6	reservoir	46.0
appreciation	47.8	bid	47.2	shady	46.6	slash	46.0
attach	47.8	courtesy	47.2	tow	46.6	stairway	46.0
axle	47.8	iceberg	47.2	astonishment	46.5	stitch	46.0
carnival	47.8	magician	47.2	coward	46.5	sway	46.0
junk	47.8	omit	47.2	disagree	46.5	swear	46.0
strictly	47.8	quotient	47.2	enjoyable	46.5	thorn	46.0
allowance	47.7	recipe	47.2	idle	46.5	arch	45.9
aye	47.7	spiral	47.2	incorrect	46.5	behold	45.9
bulletin	47.7	suitcase	47.2	intend	46.5	chariot	45.9
concentration	47.7	athlete	47.1	lily	46.5	deserve	45.9
horror	47.7	China	47.1	mittens	46.5	gloom	45.9
pearl	47.7	glare	47.1	owe	46.5	parachute	45.9
runaway	47.7	shawl	47.1	pavement	46.5	snug	45.9
surround	47.7	swollen	47.1	stroll	46.5	unbroken	45.9
vinegar	47.7	tramp	47.1	airline	46.4	dental	45.8
ankle	47.6	blaze	47.0	booth	46.4	gracious	45.8
compose	47.6	cupboard	47.0	discipline	46.4	knit	45.8
furious	47.6	dependable	47.0	dome	46.4	notch	45.8
harpoon	47.6	doubtful	47.0	hardware	46.4	Orient	45.8
phonograph	47.6	painful	47.0	harmless	46.4	penetrate	45.8
punch	47.6	plum	47.0	jack	46.4	porcupine	45.8
subway	47.6	plump	47.0	pineapple	46.4	synonym	45.8
suggestion	47.6	salary	47.0	coyote	46.3	thud	45.8
algae	47.5	stallion	47.0	hoe	46.3	anniversary	45.7
amusement	47.5	applause	46.9	homemade	46.3	budget	45.7
appetite	47.5	auto	46.9	lame	46.3	freshman	45.7
brightness	47.5	blacksmith	46.9	loan	46.3	iodine	45.7
cradle	47.5	cough	46.9	pinch	46.3	lobster	45.7
foam	47.5	deny	46.9	preposition	46.3	printer	45.7
hike	47.5	elegant	46.9	swimmer	46.3	producer	45.7
inning	47.5	gallop	46.9	auditorium	46.2	skinny	45.7
launch	47.5	gym	46.9	buoy	46.2	tumble	45.7
loom	47.5	ostrich	46.9	businessman	46.2	clatter	45.6
pebble	47.5	sting	46.9	dove	46.2	clutch	45.6
recover	47.5	uneasy	46.9	farmland	46.2	decorate	45.6
regret	47.5	announcement	46.8	imitation	46.2	flute	45.6
slim	47.5	awe	46.8	loaves	46.2	litter	45.6
sofa	47.5	collector	46.8	mountainside	46.2	rung	45.6
ash	47.4	exhaust	46.8	overalls	46.2	thrill	45.6
birch	47.4	flask	46.8	proofread	46.2	canary	45.5
cling	47.4	greatness	46.8	sailboat	46.2	cavern	45.5
clump	47.4	Greenland	46.8	sierra	46.2	conjunction	45.5
ferry	47.4	hesitate	46.8	ski	46.2	Memphis	45.5
humid	47.4	poultry	46.8	slab	46.2	percussion	45.5
impatient	47.4	pulley	46.8	slick	46.2	reed	45.5
lodge	47.4	shaggy	46.8	storekeeper	46.2	sandstone	45.5
perspiration	47.4	wedge	46.8	tack	46.2	sneak	45.5
quilt	47.4	abbreviation	46.7	boyhood	46.1	spit	45.5
rust	47.4	cedar	46.7	glacier	46.1	troop	45.5
shack	47.4	click	46.7	Neptune	46.1	undersea	45.5
suspicious	47.4	limp	46.7	posture	46.1	wasp	45.5
twinkle	47.4	macaroni	46.7	suck	46.1	bravery	45.4
absent	47.3	oar	46.7	tricky	46.1	disguise	45.4

Fourth Grade

Word		Word		Word		Word	
hymn	45.4	newborn	44.8	banjo	44.1	sly	43.6
mechanic	45.4	performer	44.8	blizzard	44.1	spectacles	43.6
missionary	45.4	sleet	44.8	cautious	44.1	twine	43.6
Providence	45.4	ballad	44.7	Harrisburg	44.1	centimeter	43.5
rattlesnake	45.4	fawn	44.7	journal	44.1	daydream	43.5
arrest	45.3	holly	44.7	packet	44.1	fling	43.5
chant	45.3	honestly	44.7	rein	44.1	gateway	43.5
colorless	45.3	intestine	44.7	rocker	44.1	paraffin	43.5
decrease	45.3	jewel	44.7	seacoast	44.1	sparrow	43.5
fungus	45.3	nibble	44.7	announcer	44.0	bough	43.4
napkin	45.3	skillet	44.7	barefoot	44.0	exponent	43.4
publish	45.3	spice	44.7	congratulations	44.0	fearless	43.4
racket	45.3	undisturbed	44.7	constellation	44.0	foghorn	43.4
sharpen	45.3	walrus	44.7	depot	44.0	redcoat	43.4
stagecoach	45.3	budge	44.6	inspector	44.0	roadway	43.4
timid	45.3	championship	44.6	interrupt	44.0	sash	43.4
torch	45.3	decoration	44.6	meteor	44.0	staple	43.4
biography	45.2	dice	44.6	unfinished	44.0	tablecloth	43.4
cod	45.2	jellyfish	44.6	vulture	44.0	wreath	43.4
courthouse	45.2	mattress	44.6	buttermilk	43.9	assortment	43.3
ignorance	45.2	miner	44.6	flip	43.9	discourage	43.3
mustache	45.2	sermon	44.6	numb	43.9	magma	43.3
spaghetti	45.2	stopper	44.6	pantry	43.9	rustle	43.3
stockade	45.2	windshield	44.6	Phoenix	43.9	sawmill	43.3
swan	45.2	dart	44.5	shipment	43.9	steeple	43.3
umpire	45.2	gong	44.5	silverware	43.9	thorax	43.3
bathe	45.1	quail	44.5	smog	43.9	burner	43.2
chapel	45.1	quiver	44.5	spat	43.9	evaporate	43.2
cooperate	45.1	sawdust	44.5	spike	43.9	math	43.2
courteous	45.1	sober	44.5	sunflower	43.9	ornament	43.2
drought	45.1	sonar	44.5	thunderstorm	43.9	roundup	43.2
groan	45.1	spur	44.5	toothpick	43.9	shortstop	43.2
hedge	45.1	telegram	44.5	alfalfa	43.8	sprout	43.2
mustard	45.1	honesty	44.4	coop	43.8	cellophane	43.1
peddler	45.1	outskirts	44.4	cot	43.8	complaint	43.1
thimble	45.1	postage	44.4	fielder	43.8	frankly	43.1
beer	45.0	afloat	44.3	hallway	43.8	respectful	43.1
coffin	45.0	brim	44.3	horseman	43.8	sweetness	43.1
crush	45.0	crate	44.3	Milwaukee	43.8	crook	43.0
dune	45.0	keyboard	44.3	oasis	43.8	groom	43.0
eagerness	45.0	lark	44.3	obedient	43.8	incoming	43.0
fee	45.0	menu	44.3	participate	43.8	luggage	43.0
inward	45.0	planetarium	44.3	rotten	43.8	skiing	43.0
shrub	45.0	Richmond	44.3	starter	43.8	squat	43.0
stride	45.0	rinse	44.3	atlas	43.7	tomahawk	43.0
treble	45.0	storehouse	44.3	chuck	43.7	turnip	43.0
vein	45.0	super	44.3	icebox	43.7	clothe	42.9
checkers	44.9	urgent	44.3	nasty	43.7	duke	42.9
congruent	44.9	await	44.2	razor	43.7	goggles	42.9
hopeful	44.9	bearded	44.2	scoop	43.7	heave	42.9
rancher	44.9	boulder	44.2	teammate	43.7	hilltop	42.9
scramble	44.9	burrow	44.2	unexpectedly	43.7	hiss	42.9
slang	44.9	bushel	44.2	whichever	43.7	smack	42.9
soften	44.9	chestnut	44.2	bandage	43.6	soggy	42.9
speck	44.9	cuckoo	44.2	banner	43.6	squaw	42.9
weatherman	44.9	elk	44.2	cottonseed	43.6	stumble	42.9
antelope	44.8	flannel	44.2	cottonwood	43.6	terrier	42.9
banquet	44.8	graveyard	44.2	frightful	43.6	tiresome	42.9
classmate	44.8	porridge	44.2	memorial	43.6	widen	42.9
Detroit	44.8	redwood	44.2	nudge	43.6	woodcutter	42.9
evaporation	44.8	regain	44.2	obedience	43.6	clothesline	42.8
mouthful	44.8	settler	44.2	pollution	43.6	duel	42.8
		wade	44.2	publisher	43.6	fuzzy	42.8
		waltz	44.2	shale	43.6	gossip	42.8

Word	Value	Word	Value	Word	Value	Word	Value
mash	42.8	senator	42.0	dizzy	41.3		
porpoise	42.8	toot	42.0	hyphen	41.3		
bully	42.7	accordion	41.9	messy	41.3	choke	40.4
dandy	42.7	brow	41.9	pickup	41.3	grunt	40.4
gulf	42.7	chirp	41.9	postmaster	41.3	housekeeper	40.4
llama	42.7	fret	41.9	siren	41.3	ignite	40.4
saucepan	42.7	gnaw	41.9	spinach	41.3	wrestle	40.4
stale	42.7	hitch	41.9	trademark	41.3	acorn	40.3
tablet	42.7	irrigate	41.9	atop	41.2	cougar	40.3
dropper	42.6	Omaha	41.9	beeswax	41.2	pinwheel	40.3
eyesight	42.6	tambourine	41.9	cinder	41.2	shuffle	40.3
lab	42.6	trio	41.9	creak	41.2	skater	40.3
likeness	42.6	wildcat	41.9	detour	41.2	veranda	40.3
receipt	42.6	alphabetically	41.8	dine	41.2	flicker	40.2
toothpaste	42.6	bulldog	41.8	dribble	41.2	geranium	40.2
wizard	42.6	fireside	41.8	flatten	41.2	lavender	40.2
caboose	42.5	moccasin	41.8	headdress	41.2	pill	40.2
chap	42.5	smokey	41.8	mermaid	41.2	chow	40.1
disorder	42.5	ambush	41.7	pickle	41.2	flier	40.1
drummer	42.5	capitol	41.7	shrug	41.2	petticoat	40.1
flare	42.5	educate	41.7	whack	41.2	pocketbook	40.1
genie	42.5	evidence	41.7	ballroom	41.1	rot	40.1
melon	42.5	harden	41.7	haystack	41.1	telltale	40.1
schoolwork	42.5	holler	41.7	huddle	41.1	wick	40.1
veil	42.5	homonym	41.7	monitor	41.1	baton	40.0
aisle	42.4	lass	41.7	needy	41.1	cirrus	40.0
driftwood	42.4	nozzle	41.7	pennant	41.1	crossbar	40.0
enlarge	42.4	prevention	41.7	poll	41.1	liar	40.0
forbid	42.4	snip	41.7	ruby	41.1	parallelogram	40.0
jealousy	42.4	carbohydrate	41.6	smother	41.1	peppermint	40.0
narrator	42.4	halo	41.6	temper	41.1	ruffle	40.0
shoreline	42.4	peacetime	41.6	upland	41.1	secrete	40.0
wasteland	42.4	quartet	41.6	jig	41.0	sheepskin	40.0
weasel	42.4	soccer	41.6	ramp	41.0	snore	40.0
blush	42.3	squirt	41.6	shorthand	41.0	wrapper	40.0
chip	42.3	strive	41.6	clarinet	40.9	battleship	39.9
comet	42.3	unsafe	41.6	clean-up	40.9	bounty	39.9
gangplank	42.3	whirlwind	41.6	apologize	40.8	buddy	39.9
hinge	42.3	assign	41.5	congressman	40.8	clang	39.9
hoof	42.3	breakdown	41.5	drawbridge	40.8	gram	39.9
pheasant	42.3	hatchet	41.5	eyelash	40.8	Hartford	39.9
poodle	42.3	lash	41.5	glitter	40.8	prowl	39.9
wee	42.3	sagebrush	41.5	plop	40.8	shopkeeper	39.9
whine	42.3	thaw	41.5	roommate	40.8	gander	39.8
antonym	42.2	whinny	41.5	batch	40.7	lipstick	39.8
chore	42.2	whitewash	41.5	eyebrow	40.7	plaza	39.8
hammock	42.2	ballplayer	41.4	hoot	40.7	ruff	39.8
lariat	42.2	cornmeal	41.4	lotion	40.7	smokestack	39.8
mummy	42.2	detergent	41.4	tablespoon	40.7	somersault	39.8
nonliving	42.2	digger	41.4	butler	40.6	trinket	39.8
bouquet	42.1	drab	41.4	cumulus	40.6	contagious	39.7
hockey	42.1	heal	41.4	noonday	40.6	cornstalk	39.7
incorrectly	42.1	manure	41.4	screwdriver	40.6	doodle	39.7
inspect	42.1	passageway	41.4	tuck	40.6	greyhound	39.7
lobby	42.1	racetrack	41.4	weaver	40.6	homespun	39.7
mister	42.1	slam	41.4	bookcase	40.5	mollusk	39.7
mitt	42.1	tong	41.4	garter	40.5	muffler	39.7
mock	42.1	villager	41.4	Jacksonville	40.5	muggy	39.7
nightmare	42.1	waterproof	41.4	latch	40.5	naughty	39.7
peck	42.1	attendance	41.3	mesa	40.5	shutter	39.7
airliner	42.0	cancel	41.3	misspell	40.5	waterfront	39.7
gauze	42.0	cigar	41.3	termite	40.5	workout	39.7
hazel	42.0	dipper	41.3	thyself	40.5	arrowhead	39.6
platter	42.0	disagreeable	41.3	tomboy	40.5	centigrade	39.6

49

Fourth Grade

fluff	39.6	playmate	38.4	lifesaving	37.4	putter	36.1
bluebird	39.5	minnow	38.3	sponsor	37.4	wildflower	36.1
freeway	39.5	spongy	38.3	tinsel	37.4	buttercup	36.0
smudge	39.5	stingy	38.3	applaud	37.3	crumb	36.0
synthesis	39.5	toothbrush	38.3	bobsled	37.3	drizzle	36.0
tricycle	39.5	corncob	38.2	indent	37.3	finch	36.0
crossword	39.4	mumble	38.2	pillar	37.3	flipper	36.0
crouch	39.4	wrestler	38.2	sandal	37.3	igloo	36.0
crowbar	39.4	candlestick	38.1	scamper	37.3	stink	36.0
goblin	39.4	clink	38.1	schoolgirl	37.3	tassel	36.0
plumber	39.4	eyelid	38.1	scooter	37.3	instruct	35.9
soothe	39.4	gurgle	38.1	stopwatch	37.3	juggler	35.9
calorie	39.3	shoeshine	38.1	thistle	37.3	patio	35.9
cookbook	39.3	strum	38.1	barbershop	37.2	seahorse	35.9
daze	39.3	apricot	38.0	mealtime	37.2	unicorn	35.9
grill	39.3	beagle	38.0	newspaperman	37.2	Wichita	35.9
ladle	39.3	crunch	38.0	windpipe	37.2	wrinkle	35.9
patent	39.3	expectant	38.0	woodshed	37.2	bodyguard	35.8
plead	39.3	greenhouse	38.0	pollute	37.1	sandstorm	35.8
polygon	39.3	postpone	38.0	smith	37.1	waken	35.8
woodsman	39.3	rainstorm	38.0	spatula	37.1	headfirst	35.7
bale	39.2	scowl	38.0	Tampa	37.1	proton	35.7
brag	39.2	scum	38.0	cowhide	37.0	sightseeing	35.7
capitalization	39.2	trapeze	38.0	Flagstaff	37.0	acrobat	35.6
foolishness	39.2	twirl	38.0	flowerpot	37.0	dewdrop	35.6
griddle	39.2	bleat	37.9	bedspread	36.9	hairpin	35.6
guppy	39.2	collie	37.9	boyfriend	36.9	quarantine	35.6
riverside	39.2	hunch	37.9	coupon	36.9	repairman	35.6
sewer	39.2	neutron	37.8	doze	36.9	shipyard	35.6
shred	39.2	seafood	37.8	lease	36.9	skid	35.6
spaniel	39.2	sift	37.8	runt	36.9	startle	35.6
wigwam	39.2	stepladder	37.8	sissy	36.9	whiff	35.6
bawl	39.1	anthem	37.7	beet	36.8	beige	35.5
jackknife	39.1	exhale	37.7	bleacher	36.8	handcuff	35.5
muffin	39.1	ooze	37.7	grate	36.8	steadfast	35.5
nonfiction	39.1	punctuate	37.7	knuckle	36.8	butte	35.3
trundle	39.1	puncture	37.7	reappear	36.8	veterinarian	35.3
aspen	39.0	summarize	37.7	roundabout	36.8	jersey	35.2
itch	39.0	tryout	37.7	stuffy	36.8	seasick	35.2
deciduous	38.9	workbench	37.7	Maypole	36.7	barrow	35.1
disappoint	38.9	bruise	37.6	meanness	36.7	boathouse	35.1
erupt	38.9	dungeon	37.6	thong	36.7	centerpiece	35.1
saxophone	38.9	nook	37.6	beanbag	36.6	tee	35.1
thicken	38.9	souvenir	37.6	ford	36.6	tomcat	35.1
churchyard	38.8	squirm	37.6	preach	36.6	trombone	35.1
kidney	38.8	twister	37.6	softball	36.6	knothole	35.0
kilometer	38.8	unselfish	37.6	almanac	36.5	matchbox	35.0
underfoot	38.8	wasteful	37.6	centipede	36.5	wallpaper	35.0
splinter	38.7	xylophone	37.6	headlight	36.5	bibliography	34.9
clasp	38.6	bedclothes	37.5	slug	36.5	drainpipe	34.9
landowner	38.6	broomstick	37.5	marketplace	36.4	foxhound	34.9
tuba	38.6	camper	37.5	spore	36.4	headstrong	34.9
clank	38.5	capillary	37.5	mug	36.3	hutch	34.9
dishonest	38.5	chug	37.5	nun	36.3	nutcracker	34.9
sag	38.5	equilateral	37.5	volleyball	36.3	toddler	34.9
waistline	38.5	grapevine	37.5	conductor	36.2	wheelchair	34.9
babble	38.4	icehouse	37.5	directory	36.2	fumble	34.8
barter	38.4	soybean	37.5	hayloft	36.2	gut	34.8
dressmaker	38.4	suntan	37.5	papoose	36.2	kimono	34.8
fisher	38.4	windstorm	37.5	scripture	36.2	tether	34.7
freezer	38.4	ark	37.4	sputter	36.2	blackbird	34.6
licorice	38.4	chubby	37.4	thumbtack	36.2	brew	34.6
		crib	37.4	dab	36.1	dung	34.6
		embarrass	37.4	ornery	36.1	getaway	34.6

glowworm	34.6	carnation	33.4	yak	31.3			**Fourth Grade**	
marmalade	34.6	fishhook	33.4	bombshell	31.1				
toadstool	34.6	deadline	33.2	tardy	31.1			rattletrap	29.6
slacks	34.5	goldsmith	33.2	burp	31.0			thundershower	29.6
snicker	34.4	spook	33.1	doorkeeper	31.0			washbowl	29.6
quadrilateral	34.3	polka	33.0	kindhearted	31.0			noodles	29.0
oboe	34.1	catsup	32.8	parkway	30.8			shampoo	29.0
yap	34.1	schoolmate	32.7	washroom	30.8			skyrocket	29.0
cartwheel	34.0	alp	32.6	airship	30.7			wristwatch	28.7
doorman	34.0	snooze	32.6	poncho	30.7			muff	28.6
downwind	34.0	waddle	32.6	tingle	30.7			piccolo	28.6
huckleberry	34.0	oriole	32.5	amaze	30.6			windowsill	28.6
juggle	34.0	housefly	32.4	displace	30.6			hobo	28.5
playroom	34.0	croak	32.3	hiccup	30.6			teepee	28.3
revoke	34.0	eyeball	32.3	locket	30.6			gumdrop	27.8
scoot	34.0	pocketknife	32.3	pigskin	30.6			setup	27.7
skein	34.0	skittish	32.3	rustler	30.6			cymbal	27.5
Toledo	34.0	terrify	32.3	snub	30.6			handwritten	27.4
wastepaper	34.0	washbasin	32.3	beanstalk	30.5			casserole	26.5
backbreaking	33.9	Topeka	32.2	cloakroom	30.5			kilogram	26.5
caramel	33.9	patrolman	32.1	mutt	30.5			tidewater	26.4
cornhusk	33.9	slop	32.0	schoolbook	30.5			hubbub	26.3
goldenrod	33.9	townsfolk	32.0	sideburns	30.5			bricklayer	26.0
junkyard	33.9	nationwide	31.9	storyteller	30.5			petunia	26.0
munch	33.9	accuse	31.8	thereon	30.5			tab	25.6
janitor	33.7	vet	31.8	typist	30.5			stupidity	25.5
lope	33.7	aspirin	31.7	freckle	30.4			girlfriend	25.1
moonbeam	33.7	downpour	31.7	pigsty	30.4			gatepost	24.6
pigtail	33.7	glisten	31.7	mid	30.2			speedway	24.6
tableware	33.7	magnify	31.5	droplet	29.9			nightshirt	23.7
cowherd	33.6	tom-tom	31.5	hailstone	29.9			rosebud	23.4
lawmaking	33.6	glaze	31.4	sherbet	29.9			savior	23.4
spangle	33.6	pixy	31.4	calfskin	29.6			typewrite	23.4
violet	33.6	tennis	31.4	frustrate	29.6			parable	23.2
washboard	33.6	drape	31.3	homecoming	29.6			pollinate	23.2
wicker	33.6	hailstorm	31.3	locksmith	29.6			thumbnail	18.8
cello	33.5	threadlike	31.3	pitch	29.6				

Word		Word		Word		Word	
arms	60.5	income	54.5	permanent	52.6	gravel	51.3
bear	59.8	negative	54.5	Israel	52.5	investigation	51.3
capital	59.5	primitive	54.5	mechanical	52.5	automatic	51.2
include	59.1	powder	54.4	nevertheless	52.5	axis	51.2
compare	58.9	previous	54.4	tense	52.5	display	51.2
process	58.9	principle	54.3	uranium	52.5	distinguish	51.2
develop	58.1	vertical	54.3	westward	52.5	fertile	51.2
variety	58.1	diameter	54.2	bacteria	52.4	horizon	51.2
solution	57.8	duty	54.2	demand	52.4	issue	51.2
rate	57.7	typical	54.2	concern	52.3	justice	51.2
mass	57.5	widely	54.2	frontier	52.3	theme	51.2
charter	57.3	former	54.1	merchant	52.3	vessel	51.2
instance	57.2	accurate	54.0	vary	52.3	vision	51.2
angle	57.1	chamber	54.0	wine	52.3	ashore	51.1
source	57.1	interior	54.0	assume	52.2	mankind	51.1
destructive	57.0	prime	54.0	authority	52.2	minister	51.1
rouge	57.0	appropriate	53.9	conflict	52.2	reflect	51.1
vast	57.0	attempt	53.9	pace	52.2	traditional	51.1
political	56.8	constant	53.9	speaker	52.2	violent	51.1
style	56.8	require	53.9	circuit	52.1	astronaut	51.0
expression	56.7	discussion	53.8	counsel	52.1	connect	51.0
composition	56.6	canal	53.7	obviously	52.1	defeat	51.0
price	56.6	essential	53.7	timber	52.1	obvious	51.0
local	56.5	slope	53.7	election	52.0	sketch	51.0
posh	56.5	species	53.7	seriously	52.0	density	50.9
determine	56.4	tobacco	53.7	cargo	51.9	harness	50.9
parallel	56.4	contrast	53.6	afterwards	51.8	rank	50.9
recent	56.2	official	53.6	formal	51.8	absolute	50.8
function	56.1	recall	53.6	international	51.8	failure	50.8
slightly	56.1	tremendous	53.5	attractive	51.7	grave	50.8
spirit	56.0	device	53.4	cannon	51.7	purchase	50.8
supplies	56.0	equivalent	53.4	credit	51.7	secure	50.8
physical	55.9	fever	53.4	economy	51.7	barely	50.7
quality	55.9	otherwise	53.4	expedition	51.7	endless	50.7
identify	55.8	suitable	53.4	latter	51.7	explosion	50.7
term	55.8	characteristic	53.3	overcome	51.7	investigate	50.7
account	55.6	formula	53.3	release	51.7	latitude	50.7
available	55.6	largely	53.3	site	51.7	link	50.7
due	55.6	project	53.3	tissue	51.7	photograph	50.7
disease	55.4	data	53.2	vacuum	51.7	photography	50.7
environment	55.4	presence	53.2	contract	51.6	quantity	50.7
musical	55.4	ain't	53.1	freight	51.6	rim	50.7
differ	55.3	independence	53.1	personality	51.6	university	50.7
complex	55.2	treatment	53.1	splendid	51.6	camel	50.6
influence	55.2	brilliant	53.0	stress	51.6	petroleum	50.6
combine	55.1	claim	53.0	survive	51.6	presently	50.6
operation	55.1	conclusion	53.0	bass	51.5	prey	50.6
production	55.1	role	53.0	concrete	51.5	stern	50.6
refer	55.1	advance	52.9	existence	51.5	alcohol	50.5
theory	55.1	apply	52.9	historical	51.5	civil	50.5
gain	55.0	comparison	52.9	illustration	51.5	grasp	50.5
review	54.9	equation	52.9	inland	51.5	midst	50.5
tax	54.9	professional	52.9	peculiar	51.5	distinct	50.4
normal	54.8	occasion	52.8	target	51.5	intersection	50.4
outline	54.8	portion	52.8	agent	51.4	mainland	50.4
affect	54.7	responsibility	52.8	countryside	51.4	precise	50.4
military	54.7	contact	52.7	efficient	51.4	risk	50.4
obtain	54.7	delicate	52.7	fond	51.4	rugged	50.4
percent	54.7	moreover	52.7	molecule	51.4	aircraft	50.3
society	54.7	federal	52.6	outstanding	51.4	countless	50.3
origin	54.6	illustrate	52.6	severe	51.4	emphasis	50.3
perform	54.6	literature	52.6	shark	51.4	hurricane	50.3

knight	50.3	marvelous	49.5	conquer	48.7	**Fifth Grade**	
mercury	50.3	profit	49.5	determination	48.7		
network	50.3	candidate	49.4	funnel	48.7	fighter	48.0
outward	50.3	classify	49.4	initial	48.7	linen	48.0
unfortunately	50.3	democracy	49.4	mantel	48.7	transport	48.0
eastward	50.2	entertainment	49.4	marsh	48.7	vermilion	48.0
formation	50.2	granite	49.4	satisfactory	48.7	association	47.9
genius	50.2	incident	49.4	sodium	48.7	conclude	47.9
limbs	50.2	intensity	49.4	southeastern	48.7	confident	47.9
lining	50.2	legal	49.4	stanza	48.7	disk	47.9
perpendicular	50.2	miracle	49.4	walnut	48.7	longitude	47.9
sacred	50.2	proceed	49.4	cabinet	48.6	tourist	47.9
scarce	50.2	savage	49.4	farewell	48.6	vitamin	47.9
scheme	50.2	vain	49.4	grim	48.6	widespread	47.9
skull	50.2	consideration	49.3	incomplete	48.6	amazement	47.8
southward	50.2	cubic	49.3	republic	48.6	bugle	47.8
verse	50.2	draft	49.3	sorrow	48.6	cloak	47.8
abroad	50.1	furnish	49.3	trout	48.6	manufacturer	47.8
leadership	50.1	peninsula	49.3	weave	48.6	refuge	47.8
opera	50.1	radius	49.3	encourage	48.5	relay	47.8
poisonous	50.1	reverse	49.3	knob	48.5	thereby	47.8
shaft	50.1	roughly	49.3	lend	48.5	tornado	47.8
treaty	50.1	conscious	49.2	naval	48.5	uncertain	47.8
province	50.0	decay	49.2	resist	48.5	acceptable	47.7
segment	50.0	demonstrate	49.2	starch	48.5	analyze	47.7
strain	50.0	fiddle	49.2	circumference	48.4	artistic	47.7
vital	50.0	foundation	49.2	parlor	48.4	meantime	47.7
arrival	49.9	locomotive	49.2	reproduce	48.4	spiritual	47.7
automatically	49.9	noble	49.2	suspect	48.4	spruce	47.7
receiver	49.9	procession	49.2	sympathy	48.4	witness	47.7
armor	49.8	scarlet	49.2	threat	48.4	ambition	47.6
capacity	49.8	solemn	49.2	vibration	48.4	barber	47.6
geometry	49.8	technology	49.2	zinc	48.4	grove	47.6
historic	49.8	abundance	49.1	coil	48.3	involve	47.6
keen	49.8	contribution	49.1	fractional	48.3	loyal	47.6
mountainous	49.8	frequent	49.1	maiden	48.3	mature	47.6
priest	49.8	interpret	49.1	muscular	48.3	miniature	47.6
shield	49.8	marine	49.1	payment	48.3	murder	47.6
survey	49.8	preserve	49.1	strengthen	48.3	ownership	47.6
tradition	49.8	accompany	49.0	debt	48.2	stock	47.6
weapon	49.8	auxiliary	49.0	delay	48.2	calcium	47.5
arc	49.7	chairman	49.0	dusk	48.2	diagonal	47.5
attraction	49.7	constitution	49.0	impulse	48.2	downstream	47.5
boom	49.7	domestic	49.0	missile	48.2	fatal	47.5
fantastic	49.7	exhausted	49.0	molasses	48.2	graduate	47.5
fate	49.7	glory	49.0	nowadays	48.2	legislature	47.5
recognition	49.7	insert	49.0	sensation	48.2	modify	47.5
sickness	49.7	possessive	49.0	tour	48.2	panic	47.5
triumph	49.7	ceremony	48.9	crest	48.1	stray	47.5
victim	49.7	league	48.9	desirable	48.1	tidal	47.5
acre	49.6	occupy	48.9	dominant	48.1	crane	47.4
chemistry	49.6	recreation	48.9	excess	48.1	fig	47.4
commerce	49.6	session	48.9	guilty	48.1	incredible	47.4
dissolve	49.6	yield	48.9	halt	48.1	lover	47.4
politics	49.6	dignity	48.8	motionless	48.1	replacement	47.4
protein	49.6	fare	48.8	musician	48.1	studio	47.4
resemble	49.6	gauge	48.8	oyster	48.1	trumpet	47.4
reveal	49.6	instinct	48.8	panel	48.1	accomplish	47.3
temporary	49.6	mare	48.8	static	48.1	apt	47.3
undoubtedly	49.6	nectar	48.8	astronomy	48.0	circulation	47.3
vivid	49.6	neutral	48.8	bait	48.0	expense	47.3
basically	49.5	northward	48.8	breed	48.0	fiber	47.3
coconut	49.5	poverty	48.8	consult	48.0	horrible	47.3
focus	49.5	clause	48.7	convention	48.0	hostile	47.3

53

Fifth Grade

word	value	word	value	word	value	word	value
productive	47.3	accordingly	46.6	gleam	46.1	collective	45.6
reflection	47.3	adequate	46.6	loft	46.1	corridor	45.6
spine	47.3	adobe	46.6	loyalty	46.1	fume	45.6
ammunition	47.2	commonplace	46.6	mercy	46.1	lung	45.6
assemble	47.2	darling	46.6	mischief	46.1	reasonably	45.6
destination	47.2	northeastern	46.6	oddly	46.1	relieve	45.6
emphasize	47.2	oxide	46.6	reign	46.1	resort	45.6
essentially	47.2	raid	46.6	rubbish	46.1	scholar	45.6
glider	47.2	stunt	46.6	blunt	46.0	shortage	45.6
outcome	47.2	tribal	46.6	bulk	46.0	simplify	45.6
assist	47.1	tundra	46.6	chlorophyll	46.0	yonder	45.6
atmospheric	47.1	virus	46.6	delightful	46.0	ancestor	45.5
conference	47.1	weird	46.6	extinct	46.0	bishop	45.5
departure	47.1	woodchuck	46.6	gale	46.0	daybreak	45.5
equality	47.1	calculate	46.5	infant	46.0	diaphragm	45.5
groove	47.1	document	46.5	intake	46.0	disgrace	45.5
restore	47.1	export	46.5	membership	46.0	economics	45.5
scrap	47.1	forecast	46.5	migrate	46.0	flint	45.5
sole	47.1	fury	46.5	protractor	46.0	frantic	45.5
stake	47.1	haste	46.5	radiant	46.0	fuss	45.5
woodland	47.1	intent	46.5	revolt	46.0	hazard	45.5
affection	47.0	lest	46.5	rotate	46.0	probe	45.5
compete	47.0	polio	46.5	salute	46.0	supreme	45.5
courageous	47.0	probable	46.5	sod	46.0	swarm	45.5
hog	47.0	runway	46.5	vaccine	46.0	warehouse	45.5
mole	47.0	slot	46.5	bind	45.9	youngster	45.5
physician	47.0	summary	46.5	cavity	45.9	cellulose	45.4
tempo	47.0	toll	46.5	confuse	45.9	compute	45.4
bridle	46.9	unfortunate	46.5	distress	45.9	dugout	45.4
demonstration	46.9	vigor	46.5	expanse	45.9	fable	45.4
foul	46.9	access	46.4	foe	45.9	fragrant	45.4
govern	46.9	declare	46.4	genuine	45.9	fund	45.4
ignorant	46.9	dispute	46.4	hatred	45.9	herring	45.4
informal	46.9	galaxy	46.4	mechanism	45.9	mortal	45.4
plank	46.9	heroic	46.4	mistress	45.9	overlook	45.4
prosperous	46.9	slit	46.4	sewage	45.9	portrait	45.4
rival	46.9	textile	46.4	stationery	45.9	stirrup	45.4
summit	46.9	tragedy	46.4	stoop	45.9	sundown	45.4
thicket	46.9	biology	46.3	unchanged	45.9	tile	45.4
upstream	46.9	brittle	46.3	underside	45.9	tilt	45.4
urban	46.9	cancer	46.3	bluff	45.8	dynamite	45.3
curb	46.8	enthusiastic	46.3	buck	45.8	hoarse	45.3
elect	46.8	import	46.3	crater	45.8	muzzle	45.3
employ	46.8	lightweight	46.3	dike	45.8	nuclei	45.3
legislative	46.8	plague	46.3	filter	45.8	overboard	45.3
monument	46.8	plaque	46.3	fragrance	45.8	partnership	45.3
plunge	46.8	rowboat	46.3	haze	45.8	plywood	45.3
reliable	46.8	terrain	46.3	hearth	45.8	ravine	45.3
reproduction	46.8	tidy	46.3	reserve	45.8	senior	45.3
surgery	46.8	totally	46.3	tangle	45.8	townspeople	45.3
translate	46.8	urge	46.3	toil	45.8	trapper	45.3
boiler	46.7	earnest	46.2	tomb	45.8	triumphant	45.3
combat	46.7	generator	46.2	waterway	45.8	assure	45.2
dye	46.7	ignore	46.2	chlorine	45.7	cultivation	45.2
frail	46.7	luxury	46.2	criticism	45.7	decline	45.2
imaginative	46.7	northwestern	46.2	envy	45.7	dolphin	45.2
inspection	46.7	quartz	46.2	faithful	45.7	geology	45.2
license	46.7	rotation	46.2	mathematician	45.7	nightfall	45.2
pouch	46.7	southwestern	46.2	mustn't	45.7	opponent	45.2
profession	46.7	surf	46.2	quarterback	45.7	rudder	45.2
thereafter	46.7	tar	46.2	seaport	45.7	sculpture	45.2
wit	46.7	unite	46.2	terrific	45.7	spout	45.2
		cease	46.1	tuna	45.7	starboard	45.2
		detect	46.1	calico	45.6	temperate	45.2

Word		Word		Word		Word	
advertise	45.1	campus	44.5	remarkably	44.0	**Fifth Grade**	
advertisement	45.1	census	44.5	silicon	44.0		
arena	45.1	eerie	44.5	trigger	44.0	immune	43.6
attain	45.1	exaggeration	44.5	uproar	44.0	monastery	43.6
backbone	45.1	geographical	44.5	affectionate	43.9	observatory	43.6
buckskin	45.1	habitat	44.5	battlefield	43.9	parchment	43.6
citrus	45.1	inform	44.5	brood	43.9	beech	43.5
foreman	45.1	rumble	44.5	collapse	43.9	condense	43.5
prickly	45.1	squadron	44.5	composite	43.9	generate	43.5
pursue	45.1	superstition	44.5	healthful	43.9	injure	43.5
thigh	45.1	transistor	44.5	impress	43.9	jest	43.5
thrive	45.1	workshop	44.5	nigh	43.9	modifier	43.5
abandon	45.0	antler	44.4	octopus	43.9	namely	43.5
adapt	45.0	charity	44.4	parakeet	43.9	offset	43.5
adventurous	45.0	employment	44.4	peer	43.9	patriotic	43.5
algebra	45.0	episode	44.4	porous	43.9	peat	43.5
alloy	45.0	hump	44.4	rabies	43.9	reaper	43.5
altar	45.0	liner	44.4	slaughter	43.9	render	43.5
consistent	45.0	newcomer	44.4	stimulus	43.9	sandpaper	43.5
exterior	45.0	outlaw	44.4	throng	43.9	seaman	43.5
fortress	45.0	panther	44.4	undergrowth	43.9	shriek	43.5
gross	45.0	promote	44.4	withstand	43.9	squad	43.5
snout	45.0	spool	44.4	ammonia	43.8	stab	43.5
accomplishment	44.9	embarrassment	44.3	binoculars	43.8	superb	43.5
comedy	44.9	heir	44.3	blubber	43.8	superlative	43.5
dismal	44.9	sedimentary	44.3	cafeteria	43.8	testimony	43.5
eel	44.9	tactics	44.3	caravan	43.8	cruise	43.4
geographic	44.9	triple	44.3	chisel	43.8	cushion	43.4
rebel	44.9	butt	44.2	clad	43.8	dagger	43.4
skipper	44.9	dwelling	44.2	cove	43.8	honeydew	43.4
stadium	44.9	eclipse	44.2	dreary	43.8	motto	43.4
voluntary	44.9	flax	44.2	durable	43.8	outlet	43.4
withdraw	44.9	politician	44.2	enclose	43.8	rickety	43.4
worthless	44.9	quill	44.2	fabulous	43.8	scorn	43.4
artery	44.8	revise	44.2	jealous	43.8	shudder	43.4
baggage	44.8	slat	44.2	landlord	43.8	tribute	43.4
cinnamon	44.8	slate	44.2	lyric	43.8	demon	43.3
compartment	44.8	snare	44.2	mammoth	43.8	descend	43.3
exclamation	44.8	sympathetic	44.2	overland	43.8	fang	43.3
honorable	44.8	takeoff	44.2	pry	43.8	mellow	43.3
interview	44.8	brace	44.1	quaint	43.8	mite	43.3
lecture	44.8	carefree	44.1	threaten	43.8	neon	43.3
mansion	44.8	chess	44.1	wail	43.8	participle	43.3
manual	44.8	coke	44.1	wreckage	43.8	profile	43.3
metropolitan	44.8	delta	44.1	wretched	43.8	saint	43.3
monarch	44.8	gunpowder	44.1	advise	43.7	scan	43.3
allegiance	44.7	hazardous	44.1	blindness	43.7	accidental	43.2
Cleveland	44.7	hydroelectric	44.1	celestial	43.7	antique	43.2
cockpit	44.7	memorable	44.1	compliment	43.7	fringe	43.2
cosmetics	44.7	offshore	44.1	employee	43.7	hark	43.2
doubtless	44.7	staircase	44.1	fragment	43.7	Indianapolis	43.2
fore	44.7	stimulate	44.1	gratitude	43.7	insult	43.2
midway	44.7	antibiotics	44.0	grope	43.7	leash	43.2
strategy	44.7	cider	44.0	inferior	43.7	linear	43.2
trough	44.7	Cincinnati	44.0	rearrange	43.7	penicillin	43.2
wartime	44.7	conserve	44.0	screech	43.7	recommend	43.2
cruelty	44.6	dissatisfied	44.0	suite	43.7	vault	43.2
cultivate	44.6	fabric	44.0	symmetry	43.7	void	43.2
gland	44.6	founder	44.0	thermal	43.7	warlike	43.2
grandstand	44.6	gem	44.0	trench	43.7	berth	43.1
Iran	44.6	hummingbird	44.0	anteater	43.6	biscuit	43.1
schoolmaster	44.6	mouthpiece	44.0	bustle	43.6	digest	43.1
turf	44.6	peg	44.0	damn	43.6	dope	43.1
bleak	44.5	recorder	44.0	decent	43.6	employer	43.1

55

Fifth Grade

install	43.1	geological	42.6	northernmost	42.1	divorce	41.4
mob	43.1	hare	42.6	serene	42.1	emerald	41.4
script	43.1	infantry	42.6	underdeveloped	42.1	enrich	41.4
underbrush	43.1	phosphate	42.6	bosom	42.0	guilt	41.4
usefulness	43.1	proclamation	42.6	dispatch	42.0	humus	41.4
vent	43.1	Springfield	42.6	heroine	42.0	lioness	41.4
cafe	43.0	vanish	42.6	manor	42.0	loudspeaker	41.4
complexion	43.0	wren	42.6	qualify	42.0	refreshment	41.4
emblem	43.0	canopy	42.5	wintry	42.0	sieve	41.4
explode	43.0	clinic	42.5	airfield	41.9	sincere	41.4
hickory	43.0	confess	42.5	criticize	41.9	sterile	41.4
merit	43.0	congress	42.5	droop	41.9	uneducated	41.4
mink	43.0	embrace	42.5	expose	41.9	blur	41.3
pueblo	43.0	glee	42.5	innocence	41.9	brotherhood	41.3
ranger	43.0	hardwood	42.5	juvenile	41.9	courtroom	41.3
silt	43.0	orphan	42.5	plunder	41.9	forge	41.3
somber	43.0	pumice	42.5	reckless	41.9	outpost	41.3
tariff	43.0	repay	42.5	resin	41.9	plume	41.3
typically	43.0	theater	42.5	slum	41.9	speedometer	41.3
candlelight	42.9	ban	42.4	birthplace	41.8	stilt	41.3
crayfish	42.9	beacon	42.4	clan	41.8	subset	41.3
designer	42.9	bog	42.4	embroidery	41.8	tinkle	41.3
dialect	42.9	halter	42.4	gutter	41.8	airtight	41.2
discount	42.9	molecular	42.4	howdy	41.8	bedrock	41.2
epidemic	42.9	obstacle	42.4	ion	41.8	brute	41.2
integer	42.9	stricken	42.4	pierce	41.8	flatter	41.2
manganese	42.9	trillion	42.4	sunup	41.8	landmark	41.2
pointer	42.9	yacht	42.4	thatch	41.8	Montgomery	41.2
broadly	42.8	clamp	42.3	tumor	41.8	saloon	41.2
broth	42.8	cleanliness	42.3	amendment	41.7	stampede	41.2
divisible	42.8	confirm	42.3	attorney	41.7	wand	41.2
edition	42.8	fleece	42.3	bunkhouse	41.7	whist	41.2
headache	42.8	flick	42.3	carp	41.7	appropriately	41.1
hexagon	42.8	hourglass	42.3	codfish	41.7	bellow	41.1
instructor	42.8	hue	42.3	landlady	41.7	conceal	41.1
locust	42.8	lightness	42.3	paddy	41.7	cornbread	41.1
mustang	42.8	nominate	42.3	rebuild	41.7	declaration	41.1
oncoming	42.8	pipeline	42.3	repel	41.7	doom	41.1
porcelain	42.8	prop	42.3	slack	41.7	heathen	41.1
preview	42.8	snarl	42.3	comprehend	41.6	inlet	41.1
ridicule	42.8	swoop	42.3	discomfort	41.6	parliament	41.1
saliva	42.8	virgin	42.3	grub	41.6	pigment	41.1
wavelength	42.8	zigzag	42.3	keg	41.6	porthole	41.1
betray	42.7	amber	42.2	linoleum	41.6	retina	41.1
boomerang	42.7	canteen	42.2	shipbuilding	41.6	shank	41.1
bulge	42.7	choppy	42.2	spurt	41.6	stovepipe	41.1
chrome	42.7	constitutional	42.2	stereo	41.6	ebb	41.0
darken	42.7	counterfeit	42.2	vow	41.6	feminine	41.0
gallant	42.7	curse	42.2	filthy	41.5	hoist	41.0
gust	42.7	exceed	42.2	ideally	41.5	millionaire	41.0
kelp	42.7	global	42.2	laurel	41.5	nag	41.0
linger	42.7	kayak	42.2	perish	41.5	pope	41.0
mourn	42.7	miraculous	42.2	pore	41.5	preferably	41.0
pinto	42.7	roost	42.2	radiate	41.5	pregnant	41.0
publication	42.7	shotgun	42.2	resent	41.5	pro	41.0
radium	42.7	sorrowful	42.2	shilling	41.5	teamwork	41.0
sediment	42.7	unimportant	42.2	slay	41.5	ambassador	40.9
slogan	42.7	appliance	42.1	starlight	41.5	catalogue	40.9
suburb	42.7	chute	42.1	stub	41.5	clash	40.9
bob	42.6	cobbler	42.1	topsoil	41.5	crumble	40.9
commotion	42.6	drake	42.1	wallet	41.5	fracas	40.9
foreigner	42.6	hopper	42.1	cartridge	41.4	geyser	40.9
		kinetic	42.1	chaps	41.4	handmade	40.9
		mischievous	42.1	crutch	41.4	intellect	40.9

ovary	40.9	thereof	40.4	stud	39.8	**Fifth Grade**	
panorama	40.9	wanderer	40.4	totem	39.8		
revolver	40.9	watertight	40.4	trustworthy	39.8	diagnose	39.0
safeguard	40.9	bail	40.3	viewpoint	39.8	filth	39.0
scurvy	40.9	cartilage	40.3	warpath	39.8	flimsy	39.0
skier	40.9	closeness	40.3	whereby	39.8	garrison	39.0
skit	40.9	disbelief	40.3	eyepiece	39.7	gazelle	39.0
slingshot	40.9	homestead	40.3	reap	39.7	longtime	39.0
suitor	40.9	nutrition	40.3	autobiography	39.6	loot	39.0
bareback	40.8	offstage	40.3	avalanche	39.6	opener	39.0
bitterness	40.8	roan	40.3	blonde	39.6	scoff	39.0
chat	40.8	spokesman	40.3	dispose	39.6	azure	38.9
competent	40.8	suicide	40.3	fraternity	39.6	fairness	38.9
eaves	40.8	wrestling	40.3	knack	39.6	forlorn	38.9
flatboat	40.8	amphibian	40.2	mucus	39.6	handicap	38.9
inhabit	40.8	breastbone	40.2	navigate	39.6	mar	38.9
inhale	40.8	flounder	40.2	rap	39.6	meteorologist	38.9
Louisville	40.8	gorge	40.2	turban	39.6	pelt	38.9
marines	40.8	implement	40.2	unsettled	39.6	secondhand	38.9
rascal	40.8	plaid	40.2	warp	39.6	sincerity	38.9
crag	40.7	pliers	40.2	yelp	39.6	springboard	38.9
henceforth	40.7	rash	40.2	cue	39.5	unskilled	38.9
homely	40.7	suds	40.2	deafening	39.5	verify	38.9
murky	40.7	tinder	40.2	grieve	39.5	anticipate	38.8
octave	40.7	troupe	40.2	livelihood	39.5	castanets	38.8
perspire	40.7	aroma	40.1	pastry	39.5	chum	38.8
shear	40.7	bronco	40.1	smelt	39.5	conveyor	38.8
shingle	40.7	Cheyenne	40.1	voter	39.5	ecology	38.8
sling	40.7	cuff	40.1	congratulate	39.4	firearms	38.8
streetcar	40.7	majesty	40.1	dedicate	39.4	foolhardy	38.8
sulfuric	40.7	prick	40.1	foster	39.4	invest	38.8
tributary	40.7	pulpit	40.1	herdsman	39.4	rubble	38.8
vanilla	40.7	rejoice	40.1	laborer	39.4	ruddy	38.8
aborigine	40.6	rumor	40.1	moisten	39.4	unbearable	38.8
antenna	40.6	rustic	40.1	prune	39.4	wring	38.8
bannister	40.6	spherical	40.1	puny	39.4	concave	38.7
cask	40.6	squall	40.1	subscribe	39.4	dame	38.7
crescent	40.6	surveyor	40.1	truthfully	39.4	drawl	38.7
cyclone	40.6	warship	40.1	asbestos	39.3	drawstring	38.7
municipal	40.6	abuse	40.0	bullfight	39.3	earshot	38.7
shun	40.6	beta	40.0	burr	39.3	latex	38.7
sire	40.6	clamor	40.0	chopsticks	39.3	Nashville	38.7
vaccination	40.6	colon	40.0	inventory	39.3	songbird	38.7
wardrobe	40.6	easel	40.0	loam	39.3	tugboat	38.7
appoint	40.5	mute	40.0	lye	39.3	unwind	38.7
audible	40.5	parasol	40.0	mantelpiece	39.3	bonny	38.6
catastrophe	40.5	rump	40.0	silversmith	39.3	cranny	38.6
dismiss	40.5	stead	40.0	strife	39.3	gush	38.6
garlic	40.5	tidings	40.0	usher	39.3	khaki	38.6
nomadic	40.5	administer	39.9	attendant	39.2	lawful	38.6
parasite	40.5	congregation	39.9	crackle	39.2	Portland	38.6
propel	40.5	crease	39.9	curd	39.2	romp	38.6
rout	40.5	dude	39.9	devour	39.2	roster	38.6
skyline	40.5	flaw	39.9	federation	39.2	standstill	38.6
varnish	40.5	hedgehog	39.9	pod	39.2	vineyard	38.6
witchcraft	40.5	incline	39.9	poker	39.2	clockwork	38.5
convex	40.4	inspire	39.9	seller	39.2	dangle	38.5
easygoing	40.4	mortgage	39.9	torpedo	39.2	hereby	38.5
firelight	40.4	putty	39.9	downright	39.1	inquire	38.5
muskrat	40.4	saucy	39.9	overcast	39.1	molt	38.5
nitrate	40.4	waterfowl	39.9	purify	39.1	submerge	38.5
premium	40.4	bloodshed	39.8	stockyard	39.1	withhold	38.5
puritan	40.4	horde	39.8	twang	39.1	chowder	38.4
sanitary	40.4	medley	39.8	blunder	39.0	circulate	38.4

Fifth Grade

word	value	word	value	word	value	word	value
colonist	38.4	ceramic	37.7	clot	36.8	spire	36.1
hogan	38.4	chrysanthemum	37.7	couch	36.8	backstop	36.0
subheading	38.4	exaggerate	37.7	crotch	36.8	cockroach	36.0
thunderbolt	38.4	fray	37.7	diploma	36.8	daredevil	36.0
tuft	38.4	grindstone	37.7	ferment	36.8	hamper	36.0
duet	38.3	lair	37.7	handbook	36.8	handshake	36.0
dwindle	38.3	pastime	37.7	intersect	36.8	ointment	36.0
eventual	38.3	rehearse	37.7	jogging	36.8	plod	36.0
honeysuckle	38.3	rind	37.7	Lansing	36.8	powwow	36.0
insofar	38.3	whereabouts	37.7	meek	36.8	quirk	36.0
rookie	38.3	brighten	37.6	picker	36.8	raven	36.0
scuffle	38.3	crumple	37.6	silkworm	36.8	refuel	36.0
sportsman	38.3	lengthen	37.6	sprawl	36.8	regal	36.0
sprint	38.3	mason	37.6	windbreak	36.8	ruckus	36.0
stomp	38.3	mimic	37.6	clutter	36.7	shin	36.0
wayside	38.3	ornate	37.6	doe	36.7	slump	36.0
arbor	38.2	prophet	37.6	fathom	36.7	tint	36.0
armchair	38.2	scourge	37.6	grime	36.7	topside	36.0
curriculum	38.2	sheath	37.6	grower	36.7	trooper	36.0
dogwood	38.2	swap	37.6	scrawny	36.7	witty	36.0
frolic	38.2	tempest	37.6	someway	36.7	blockhouse	35.9
muster	38.2	watercolor	37.6	uncontrolled	36.7	coax	35.9
opal	38.2	whittle	37.6	wart	36.7	hobble	35.9
peal	38.2	wither	37.6	bloodstream	36.6	horrify	35.9
pep	38.2	pun	37.5	browse	36.6	landslide	35.9
relish	38.2	downfall	37.4	embankment	36.6	mockingbird	35.9
stoke	38.2	dweller	37.4	kiln	36.6	pastor	35.9
sunfish	38.2	eternity	37.4	lattice	36.6	slosh	35.9
throb	38.2	snapper	37.4	milkweed	36.6	surfboard	35.9
twitch	38.2	sundial	37.4	penmanship	36.6	attire	35.8
washtub	38.2	footwear	37.3	pygmy	36.6	lighten	35.8
cinch	38.1	greenery	37.3	strangle	36.6	notify	35.8
flue	38.1	haunt	37.3	unravel	36.6	alto	35.7
lunge	38.1	jiffy	37.3	woodwind	36.6	beefsteak	35.7
maize	38.1	judgment	37.3	flora	36.5	grit	35.7
nourish	38.1	lacrosse	37.3	sheaf	36.5	litmus	35.7
visor	38.1	pasteboard	37.3	tawny	36.5	stamina	35.7
backstage	38.0	sneer	37.3	vacationer	36.5	beeline	35.6
badger	38.0	toothache	37.3	whop	36.5	dues	35.6
cologne	38.0	unsteady	37.3	bravo	36.4	forklift	35.6
everlasting	38.0	waver	37.3	cameraman	36.4	logger	35.6
gruff	38.0	cutlass	37.2	pecan	36.4	lurch	35.6
lag	38.0	dungarees	37.2	primer	36.4	nostril	35.6
minuet	38.0	cuneiform	37.1	swordfish	36.4	ramshackle	35.6
obsidian	38.0	haven	37.1	battleground	36.3	slink	35.6
tart	38.0	scamp	37.1	cobblestone	36.3	stateroom	35.6
timetable	38.0	symptom	37.1	commandment	36.3	baseboard	35.5
bagpipe	37.9	dingo	37.0	falsehood	36.3	sup	35.5
malt	37.9	entertainer	37.0	gatekeeper	36.3	swash	35.5
masculine	37.9	lather	37.0	ghetto	36.3	cheesecloth	35.4
module	37.9	lawnmower	37.0	invert	36.3	lounge	35.4
palette	37.9	pounce	37.0	phantom	36.3	posse	35.4
shrewdly	37.9	sandalwood	37.0	cuticle	36.2	smokehouse	35.4
turquoise	37.9	turnover	37.0	forester	36.2	thunderhead	35.4
ware	37.9	airman	36.9	guideline	36.2	civilize	35.3
brakeman	37.8	condensation	36.9	independent	36.2	intelligible	35.3
buff	37.8	cottontail	36.9	potion	36.2	irritate	35.3
lumberjack	37.8	gloss	36.9	deceit	36.1	spyglass	35.3
northerly	37.8	headmaster	36.9	figurehead	36.1	ventriloquist	35.3
null	37.8	promenade	36.9	garland	36.1	volley	35.3
skyward	37.8	stag	36.9	horseless	36.1	basswood	35.2
snorkel	37.8	tropics	36.9	platypus	36.1	brickwork	35.2
		yearling	36.9	rawboned	36.1	decoy	35.2
		broil	36.8	spatter	36.1	headboard	35.2

pamphlet	35.2		
showman	35.2		
celebrity	35.1		
dazzle	35.1		
fluke	35.1		
salon	35.1		
snowshoe	35.1		
stile	35.1		
tatter	35.1		
buffet	35.0		
godmother	35.0		
overwhelm	35.0		
vat	35.0		
beautify	34.9		
lob	34.9		
payroll	34.9		
potter	34.9		
prescription	34.9		
applesauce	34.8		
astonish	34.8		
faction	34.8		
showdown	34.8		
yowl	34.8		
bologna	34.7		
custody	34.7		
glassware	34.7		
lopsided	34.7		
pinafore	34.7		
swagger	34.7		
tempt	34.7		
wolfhound	34.7		
yank	34.7		
fertilize	34.6		
invertebrate	34.6		
verge	34.6		
cheekbone	34.5		
lifelong	34.5		
beret	34.4		
obstruct	34.4		
tabletop	34.4		
trudge	34.4		
clothespin	34.3		
mallard	34.3		
strut	34.3		
tableland	34.3		
mayonnaise	34.2		
coliseum	34.1		
gelatin	34.1		
ping	34.1		
pith	34.1		
tang	34.1		
anyhow	34.0		
confetti	34.0		
delightfully	34.0		
magenta	34.0		
meadowlark	34.0		
Peoria	34.0		
seep	34.0		
sloppy	34.0		
wad	34.0		
airstrip	33.9		
almond	33.9		
bedroll	33.9		
blindfold	33.9		

heartbreak	33.9		
jog	33.9		
paperback	33.9		
pitchfork	33.9		
sideline	33.9		
stagehand	33.9		
tortilla	33.9		
wield	33.9		
childbearing	33.7		
diminish	33.7		
fizz	33.7		
fourscore	33.7		
heartache	33.7		
sphinx	33.7		
testament	33.7		
chessboard	33.6		
deepen	33.6		
demolish	33.6		
Duluth	33.6		
fad	33.6		
marshland	33.6		
mural	33.6		
puma	33.6		
aqueduct	33.5		
snapshot	33.5		
balsa	33.4		
millstone	33.4		
smirk	33.4		
snuggle	33.4		
underdog	33.4		
dooryard	33.3		
gel	33.3		
suede	33.3		
trice	33.3		
hilarious	33.2		
humpback	33.2		
nugget	33.2		
taffy	33.2		
launder	33.1		
brunette	33.0		
chime	33.0		
keyhole	33.0		
pharmacy	33.0		
badminton	32.9		
flabby	32.9		
sandbox	32.8		
shimmer	32.8		
talkative	32.8		
cornucopia	32.7		
pucker	32.7		
culvert	32.6		
husk	32.6		
modernize	32.6		
nutshell	32.6		
pimple	32.6		
scraper	32.4		
blister	32.3		
cloudburst	32.3		
crock	32.3		
disconnect	32.3		
skirmish	32.3		
canvas	32.2		
bareheaded	32.1		
hectic	32.1		

pug	32.1		
waterside	32.1		
cavalryman	32.0		
honeymoon	32.0		
hydrochloric	32.0		
tuber	32.0		
flair	31.9		
horseflesh	31.9		
modesty	31.9		
parole	31.9		
subsist	31.9		
smug	31.8		
exclamatory	31.7		
freak	31.7		
neigh	31.7		
signpost	31.7		
sliver	31.7		
squint	31.7		
trimmer	31.6		
larkspur	31.5		
senate	31.5		
breastplate	31.4		
drumstick	31.4		
flapjack	31.4		
jumbo	31.4		
workhouse	31.4		
bristle	31.3		
deathbed	31.3		
imp	31.3		
kitchenware	31.3		
sidetrack	31.3		
compel	31.1		
clench	31.0		
clog	31.0		
drench	31.0		
workday	30.8		
adorable	30.7		
awning	30.7		
dolt	30.7		
drainboard	30.7		
gag	30.7		
gravestone	30.7		
inkstand	30.7		
kidnap	30.7		
pellet	30.7		
polo	30.7		
spearmint	30.7		
sprig	30.7		
coy	30.6		
cringe	30.6		
dogie	30.6		
dragonfly	30.6		
duct	30.6		
excel	30.6		
frill	30.6		
groggy	30.6		
guardhouse	30.6		
rifleman	30.6		
rumpus	30.6		
scab	30.6		
scrawl	30.6		
shamble	30.6		
slush	30.6		
stagger	30.6		

Fifth Grade

thereto	30.6
tinge	30.6
tot	30.6
washstand	30.6
chef	30.5
childbirth	30.5
convict	30.5
cornet	30.5
crave	30.5
falter	30.5
fend	30.5
foothill	30.5
gob	30.5
headstone	30.5
hitchhike	30.5
jackass	30.5
lobe	30.5
manicure	30.5
stiffen	30.5
tradesman	30.5
westernmost	30.5
trill	30.4
pentagon	30.2
thresh	30.2
torchlight	30.2
wheeze	30.2
waistband	29.7
amble	29.6
bloodhound	29.6
cannonball	29.6
chalet	29.6
cistern	29.6
duchess	29.6
fidget	29.6
gardenia	29.6
handbill	29.6
hornet	29.6
jab	29.6
lumberyard	29.6
racecourse	29.6
shatter	29.6
sugarcane	29.6
sulk	29.6
tannery	29.6
thrash	29.6
turnout	29.6
washout	29.6
wrongdoing	29.6
yodel	29.6
cad	29.5
lumberman	29.1
cumulonimbus	29.0
grenade	28.6
blockhead	28.5
soapsuds	28.1
pastel	28.0
birthmark	27.8
confederacy	27.7
covey	27.7
earphone	27.7
icecap	27.7
radiophone	27.7

Fifth Grade

ragweed	27.7	chinaware	25.9	shortcut	23.9	trespass	23.4
voiceless	27.4	midwest	25.9	unattractive	23.9	brier	23.3
crescendo	26.9	vandal	25.6	wallflower	23.9	woodpile	23.3
cannibal	26.7	sultan	25.0	bluebell	23.7	equip	23.2
octagon	26.5	sportscaster	24.8	coffeepot	23.7	hunchback	23.2
belle	26.4	pillbox	24.6	gunsmith	23.7	meditate	23.2
boxwood	26.2	countryman	23.9	pudgy	23.7	depart	22.1
		nude	23.9	frontiersman	23.4	nursemaid	22.1

Sixth Grade

indicate	56.7	benefit	50.5	impressive	48.7	conscience	47.7
progress	56.0	impact	50.5	injury	48.7	consent	47.7
standard	55.5	throne	50.5	request	48.7	decade	47.7
mortar	55.1	illness	50.3	stout	48.7	erect	47.7
atomic	54.8	expansion	50.2	utmost	48.7	democratic	47.6
additional	54.7	massive	50.2	venture	48.7	oral	47.6
bound	54.7	crude	50.1	compact	48.6	weakness	47.6
eventually	54.6	irregular	50.1	composer	48.6	emotion	47.5
naturally	54.5	multiple	50.1	context	48.6	memorize	47.5
ore	54.0	barren	50.0	critical	48.6	bond	47.4
effective	53.4	competition	49.9	despair	48.6	colonel	47.4
detail	53.3	fright	49.9	graceful	48.6	conquest	47.4
thrust	53.3	vocal	49.9	identical	48.6	eliminate	47.4
unique	53.3	extraordinary	49.8	sheer	48.6	endure	47.4
trial	53.2	hence	49.8	surrender	48.6	migration	47.4
reaction	53.1	maximum	49.8	technique	48.6	poetic	47.4
apparently	53.0	predict	49.8	evident	48.5	possess	47.4
scarcely	53.0	logical	49.7	tension	48.5	sleek	47.4
rare	52.9	quotation	49.7	barley	48.4	survival	47.4
numerous	52.8	version	49.7	bolt	48.4	synthetic	47.4
soul	52.8	accustomed	49.6	destruction	48.4	twilight	47.4
majority	52.6	bearing	49.6	pulp	48.4	acquire	47.3
mate	52.6	prominent	49.5	broadcast	48.3	confederate	47.3
despite	52.5	reality	49.5	cunning	48.3	convey	47.3
generation	52.5	elaborate	49.4	contribute	48.2	dialogue	47.3
harmony	52.4	universal	49.4	percentage	48.2	meridian	47.3
impression	52.4	whereas	49.4	pork	48.2	starling	47.3
clerk	52.3	insurance	49.2	reef	48.2	acute	47.2
defense	52.3	plantation	49.2	texture	48.2	associate	47.2
continuous	51.9	radiation	49.2	likewise	48.1	organic	47.2
notation	51.7	rational	49.2	observer	48.1	ram	47.2
expand	51.6	variation	49.2	particle	48.1	tailor	47.2
fleet	51.5	retreat	49.1	peasant	48.1	villain	47.2
nerve	51.5	transparent	49.1	philosophy	48.1	ambitious	47.1
procedure	51.5	arise	49.0	visual	48.1	establishment	47.1
substitute	51.4	estate	49.0	consequently	48.0	ginger	47.1
host	51.2	extensive	49.0	convenience	48.0	interfere	47.1
plot	51.2	transfer	49.0	fundamental	48.0	reform	47.1
proportion	51.2	velocity	49.0	immense	48.0	steamboat	47.1
technical	51.2	apparatus	48.9	leisure	48.0	terminal	47.1
campaign	51.0	array	48.9	admiration	47.9	warfare	47.1
enable	50.9	evidently	48.9	alas	47.9	descent	47.0
sequence	50.9	literally	48.9	astronomer	47.9	homeland	46.9
conduct	50.8	minimum	48.9	persuade	47.9	pluck	46.9
exploration	50.8	moral	48.9	cigarette	47.8	random	46.9
marriage	50.8	span	48.9	distinctive	47.8	classification	46.8
odor	50.8	spectacular	48.9	pursuit	47.8	divine	46.8
internal	50.7	abundant	48.8	react	47.8	enterprise	46.8
achieve	50.6	membrane	48.8	adjacent	47.7	fatigue	46.8
district	50.6	reckon	48.8	amateur	47.7	piston	46.8
appeal	50.5	vigorous	48.8	classic	47.7	comparative	46.7

misery	46.7	treacherous	45.8	absurd	44.8	**Sixth Grade**	
retain	46.7	underlying	45.8	dainty	44.8		
vague	46.7	utter	45.8	hitherto	44.8	completion	44.0
chemist	46.6	criminal	45.7	pledge	44.8	compression	44.0
funeral	46.6	deed	45.7	proposal	44.8	converse	44.0
indication	46.6	digestive	45.7	surge	44.8	incredibly	44.0
insulation	46.6	elder	45.7	captive	44.7	logic	44.0
petition	46.6	liberal	45.7	clockwise	44.7	luster	44.0
spinal	46.6	madam	45.7	fulfill	44.7	realistic	44.0
subtle	46.6	maintenance	45.7	headlong	44.7	sensory	44.0
translation	46.6	majestic	45.7	sullen	44.7	superintendent	44.0
conform	46.5	malaria	45.7	conspicuous	44.6	devise	43.9
debate	46.5	organism	45.7	domain	44.6	duration	43.9
devotion	46.5	presidential	45.7	electromagnetic	44.6	fantasy	43.9
passion	46.5	sculptor	45.7	evergreen	44.6	highland	43.9
roadside	46.5	sulphur	45.7	ghostly	44.6	paradise	43.9
steamer	46.5	transform	45.7	inevitably	44.6	privacy	43.9
interval	46.4	clarity	45.6	surplus	44.6	remedy	43.9
rye	46.4	consequence	45.6	vicious	44.6	socket	43.9
suspense	46.4	emperor	45.6	abstract	44.5	supposedly	43.9
symphony	46.4	endurance	45.6	disgust	44.5	ample	43.8
unquestionably	46.4	external	45.6	gaunt	44.5	auction	43.8
anxiety	46.3	undergo	45.6	lateral	44.5	feat	43.8
apprentice	46.3	contempt	45.5	luminous	44.5	foliage	43.8
barge	46.3	customary	45.5	magical	44.5	gait	43.8
digestion	46.3	italics	45.5	mint	44.5	invade	43.8
enamel	46.3	unconscious	45.5	sacrifice	44.5	photographer	43.8
engage	46.3	architect	45.4	tournament	44.5	skeletal	43.8
infection	46.3	aviation	45.4	acquaintance	44.4	surgeon	43.8
intricate	46.3	extract	45.4	crucial	44.4	turpentine	43.8
schooner	46.3	filament	45.4	fashionable	44.4	inherit	43.7
wrought	46.3	gin	45.4	garment	44.4	installation	43.7
cathedral	46.2	marvel	45.4	offense	44.4	notably	43.7
correspondence	46.2	regulate	45.4	unlimited	44.4	rotor	43.7
dismay	46.2	revolve	45.4	discharge	44.3	symbolize	43.7
explosive	46.2	trait	45.4	feeble	44.3	taut	43.7
graduation	46.2	inexpensive	45.3	hash	44.3	uncommon	43.7
insure	46.2	overseas	45.3	hub	44.3	binary	43.6
ivory	46.2	similarity	45.3	nymph	44.3	debris	43.6
nuisance	46.2	enforce	45.2	shabby	44.3	exhaustion	43.6
seemingly	46.2	homeward	45.2	smallpox	44.3	monstrous	43.6
thorough	46.2	offspring	45.2	wary	44.3	phosphorus	43.6
valve	46.2	purely	45.2	ancestry	44.2	resolve	43.6
vicinity	46.2	simultaneously	45.2	ascent	44.2	threshold	43.6
casual	46.1	transmit	45.2	frenzy	44.2	wrath	43.6
climax	46.1	unequal	45.2	mobile	44.2	alien	43.5
energetic	46.1	worthwhile	45.2	prediction	44.2	collision	43.5
grant	46.1	alter	45.1	regiment	44.2	excerpt	43.5
jazz	46.1	revenge	45.1	representation	44.2	finance	43.5
prospect	46.1	shrine	45.1	spindle	44.2	lance	43.5
sergeant	46.1	suspicion	45.1	token	44.2	serpent	43.5
turbine	46.1	dwell	45.0	torrent	44.2	windlass	43.5
indefinite	46.0	fragile	45.0	trifle	44.2	fuse	43.4
manuscript	46.0	legendary	45.0	wilt	44.2	hospitality	43.4
overall	46.0	starvation	45.0	ally	44.1	exquisite	43.3
watchman	46.0	arouse	44.9	cock	44.1	flank	43.3
crimson	45.9	combustion	44.9	grassland	44.1	hermit	43.3
experimentation	45.9	crisis	44.9	Helena	44.1	rig	43.3
flourish	45.9	duplicate	44.9	motive	44.1	squid	43.3
prose	45.9	embryo	44.9	neglect	44.1	technically	43.3
stationary	45.9	eternal	44.9	ordeal	44.1	veteran	43.3
wage	45.9	propose	44.9	refrain	44.1	penal	43.2
category	45.8	radiator	44.9	sow	44.1	peril	43.2
perceive	45.8	sac	44.9	suspension	44.1	scroll	43.2

Sixth Grade

Word		Word		Word		Word	
authentic	43.1	derive	42.3	mythology	41.6	clement	40.7
bison	43.1	execute	42.3	perilous	41.6	contentment	40.7
gorgeous	43.1	geologist	42.3	animated	41.5	heretofore	40.7
lacquer	43.1	mutton	42.3	ballot	41.5	inert	40.7
lure	43.1	objection	42.3	behalf	41.5	musket	40.7
refinery	43.1	pedestrian	42.3	carbonate	41.5	siege	40.7
rehearsal	43.1	pitiful	42.3	eccentric	41.5	sinister	40.7
verdict	43.1	steamship	42.3	guardian	41.5	traitor	40.7
whereupon	43.1	compressor	42.2	herb	41.5	academy	40.6
wingspread	43.1	desperation	42.2	portray	41.5	mica	40.6
arid	43.0	doctrine	42.2	quote	41.5	bias	40.5
beforehand	43.0	miller	42.2	strand	41.5	countdown	40.5
gallery	43.0	warrant	42.2	tungsten	41.5	countenance	40.5
lush	43.0	accord	42.1	agile	41.4	eucalyptus	40.5
maze	43.0	aquatic	42.1	cobalt	41.4	isthmus	40.5
merchandise	43.0	bauxite	42.1	foresee	41.4	parson	40.5
commit	42.9	bracket	42.1	greed	41.4	preside	40.5
defensive	42.9	contour	42.1	hasty	41.4	sanitation	40.5
guinea	42.9	dose	42.1	hither	41.4	scornful	40.5
ironically	42.9	potassium	42.1	knoll	41.4	sinew	40.5
nonetheless	42.9	subsequently	42.1	overtake	41.4	tranquil	40.5
regulation	42.9	unstable	42.1	seam	41.4	treason	40.5
aerial	42.8	vice	42.1	tenant	41.4	tuberculosis	40.5
cutter	42.8	alternately	42.0	dingy	41.3	asphalt	40.4
fracture	42.8	brink	42.0	rightful	41.3	continual	40.4
plumb	42.8	cloves	42.0	warden	41.3	eloquent	40.4
presumably	42.8	genetic	42.0	diphtheria	41.2	hover	40.4
submit	42.8	moat	42.0	evolve	41.2	indigo	40.4
throttle	42.8	monopoly	42.0	ferryboat	41.2	inscription	40.4
torture	42.8	resolution	42.0	hostess	41.2	merge	40.4
consume	42.7	soprano	42.0	isotope	41.2	offend	40.4
disastrous	42.7	stubby	42.0	racer	41.2	pang	40.4
menace	42.7	client	41.9	scythe	41.2	propulsion	40.4
orbital	42.7	gene	41.9	whisk	41.2	supervise	40.4
abrupt	42.6	hurdle	41.9	firefly	41.1	watershed	40.4
burial	42.6	outlying	41.9	oneself	41.1	watt	40.4
corpse	42.6	riot	41.9	prosper	41.1	disturbance	40.3
ferocious	42.6	scholarship	41.9	retail	41.1	essence	40.3
monk	42.6	summon	41.9	sweetheart	41.1	liable	40.3
parsley	42.6	tangible	41.9	tallow	41.1	rouse	40.3
romance	42.6	taxation	41.9	breakthrough	41.0	shrewd	40.3
statesman	42.6	tyrant	41.9	bungalow	41.0	standpoint	40.3
thermostat	42.6	biologist	41.8	calculation	41.0	teller	40.3
tutor	42.6	collide	41.8	gadget	41.0	therapy	40.3
wholesome	42.6	discontent	41.8	nobleman	41.0	topple	40.3
woe	42.6	escort	41.8	prow	41.0	bandanna	40.2
wrench	42.6	freighter	41.8	speculate	41.0	drone	40.2
morrow	42.5	secrecy	41.8	usable	41.0	hinder	40.2
retire	42.5	spectator	41.8	valid	41.0	lyre	40.2
splint	42.5	Trenton	41.8	decree	40.9	makeshift	40.2
diesel	42.4	unrest	41.8	despise	40.9	plea	40.2
insignificant	42.4	boon	41.7	estuary	40.9	sheen	40.2
lanky	42.4	caste	41.7	idol	40.9	weariness	40.2
merciless	42.4	prompt	41.7	justly	40.9	drastic	40.1
opaque	42.4	regime	41.7	laser	40.9	hasten	40.1
overseer	42.4	steed	41.7	metamorphosis	40.9	interruption	40.1
reactor	42.4	turmoil	41.7	respiratory	40.9	pose	40.1
reciprocal	42.4	baron	41.6	tapestry	40.9	restrain	40.1
stewardess	42.4	carcass	41.6	antic	40.8	tanker	40.1
unison	42.4	con	41.6	barracks	40.8	tonic	40.1
abreast	42.3	exceptional	41.6	civic	40.8	unfit	40.1
accommodate	42.3	grotesque	41.6	graphite	40.8	vise	40.1
		hybrid	41.6	hemlock	40.8	airway	40.0
		jumble	41.6	avail	40.7	feldspar	40.0

Word		Word		Word		Word	
hammerhead	40.0	broadside	39.3	paralyze	38.6		
morsel	40.0	delegate	39.3	ratio	38.6		
quake	40.0	ecstasy	39.3	resolute	38.6	jalopy	37.7
scurry	40.0	microbe	39.3	sedan	38.6	liquor	37.7
solitude	40.0	potent	39.3	wry	38.6	listless	37.7
circulatory	39.9	robust	39.3	aimless	38.5	median	37.7
circumstance	39.9	rollicking	39.3	bisect	38.5	naive	37.7
faulty	39.9	scribe	39.3	cud	38.5	puck	37.7
improvise	39.9	trance	39.3	haughty	38.5	ruffian	37.7
momentary	39.9	whiskey	39.3	hyena	38.5	scuttle	37.7
pinpoint	39.9	alpha	39.2	inhabitant	38.5	bedlam	37.6
repeal	39.9	constable	39.2	isometric	38.5	bleach	37.6
rift	39.9	counterclockwise	39.2	mirth	38.5	chaste	37.6
attentive	39.8	glucose	39.2	outlandish	38.5	famine	37.6
dire	39.8	infer	39.2	prim	38.5	levy	37.6
frank	39.8	introductory	39.2	spade	38.5	plush	37.6
ghastly	39.8	lute	39.2	victor	38.5	republican	37.6
massacre	39.8	par	39.2	bunt	38.4	seaboard	37.6
massage	39.8	probation	39.2	bygone	38.4	serum	37.6
metaphor	39.8	specify	39.2	creed	38.4	sizzle	37.6
ransom	39.8	trample	39.2	remorse	38.4	sledge	37.6
arsenal	39.7	bran	39.1	acknowledge	38.3	stronghold	37.6
cleft	39.7	feverish	39.1	crankshaft	38.3	agility	37.5
contraption	39.7	frigid	39.1	hideous	38.3	apparel	37.5
dormant	39.7	incense	39.1	legacy	38.3	hydraulic	37.5
fallow	39.7	livid	39.1	petty	38.3	inject	37.5
invalid	39.7	overthrow	39.1	preface	38.3	legume	37.5
irritable	39.7	waistcoat	39.1	tolerance	38.3	straightforward	37.5
momentarily	39.7	bizarre	39.0	truant	38.3	suspend	37.5
refresh	39.7	impose	39.0	bowstring	38.2	tragically	37.5
shanty	39.7	infrequent	39.0	defy	38.2	vulgar	37.5
snuff	39.7	institute	39.0	grudge	38.2	conjecture	37.4
theoretically	39.7	insulator	39.0	noose	38.2	cornerstone	37.4
whilst	39.7	lagoon	39.0	nourishment	38.2	delirious	37.4
accelerate	39.6	undeniably	39.0	psalm	38.2	indicator	37.4
burly	39.6	zest	39.0	sultry	38.2	intrigue	37.4
industrious	39.6	amazingly	38.9	tribune	38.2	chauffeur	37.3
influenza	39.6	contestant	38.9	windblown	38.2	discreet	37.3
legible	39.6	crisscross	38.9	archer	38.1	floe	37.3
persist	39.6	sulfate	38.9	beset	38.1	footwork	37.3
reject	39.6	terminate	38.9	boulevard	38.1	giddy	37.3
reproductive	39.6	attribute	38.8	compress	38.1	outwit	37.3
silhouette	39.6	conceivably	38.8	mainstream	38.1	urchin	37.3
squire	39.6	gamble	38.8	oppose	38.1	adorn	37.2
astrology	39.5	grueling	38.8	protector	38.1	backwoods	37.2
exclude	39.5	honeycomb	38.8	adviser	38.0	bromine	37.2
fugitive	39.5	idiom	38.8	audio	38.0	nightcap	37.2
furrow	39.5	outboard	38.8	bachelor	38.0	teak	37.2
inertia	39.5	scoundrel	38.8	crevice	38.0	anonymous	37.1
jolt	39.5	slicker	38.8	sublime	38.0	ascend	37.1
monsoon	39.5	sophomore	38.8	diction	37.9	biceps	37.1
porter	39.5	tangerine	38.8	mince	37.9	distort	37.1
spontaneous	39.5	boycott	38.7	outrage	37.9	equilibrium	37.1
acreage	39.4	diplomat	38.7	beverage	37.8	fundamentally	37.1
camouflage	39.4	lug	38.7	blight	37.8	imprison	37.1
comprise	39.4	negotiate	38.7	dormitory	37.8	rabbi	37.1
cult	39.4	prevail	38.7	metropolis	37.8	referee	37.1
firebox	39.4	profane	38.7	notwithstanding	37.8	seminary	37.1
frogman	39.4	reliability	38.7	passport	37.8	tolerate	37.1
perishable	39.4	vigil	38.7	powerhouse	37.8	violinist	37.1
taxpayer	39.4	console	38.6	volt	37.8	homophone	37.0
teen	39.4	headway	38.6	administrator	37.7	steppe	37.0
torment	39.4	millpond	38.6	bribe	37.7	vaudeville	37.0
trolley	39.4	mosaic	38.6	eligible	37.7	astonishingly	36.9

Sixth Grade

Word	Score
champagne	36.9
condemn	36.9
croquet	36.9
legion	36.9
patriarch	36.9
sect	36.9
tribesman	36.9
villa	36.9
discard	36.8
gill	36.8
huff	36.8
silo	36.8
tier	36.8
understandably	36.8
unfavorable	36.8
blare	36.7
lull	36.7
portal	36.7
prance	36.7
slouch	36.7
tarpaulin	36.7
albatross	36.6
bowel	36.6
bureau	36.6
cascade	36.6
layout	36.6
populate	36.6
undiscovered	36.6
deft	36.5
hereafter	36.5
hygiene	36.5
impurity	36.5
jubilant	36.5
rawhide	36.5
stifle	36.5
acquaint	36.4
crossbow	36.4
encircle	36.4
guillotine	36.4
predicament	36.4
sensibly	36.4
jute	36.3
lore	36.3
shipwreck	36.3
helm	36.2
illuminate	36.2
tusk	36.2
breakneck	36.1
confer	36.1
denounce	36.1
eggplant	36.1
garb	36.1
glimmer	36.1
gnat	36.1
incentive	36.1
jinx	36.1
lapse	36.1
lichen	36.1
limelight	36.1
nausea	36.1
nip	36.1
onslaught	36.1
overwork	36.1
purge	36.1
utensil	36.1
cashier	36.0
copilot	36.0
curfew	36.0
defile	36.0
denomination	36.0
farsighted	36.0
hilt	36.0
inactive	36.0
premises	36.0
prosecute	36.0
psychiatrist	36.0
runoff	36.0
subdue	36.0
uncanny	36.0
caustic	35.9
debut	35.9
fickle	35.9
groundwork	35.9
gruel	35.9
hurl	35.9
kink	35.9
presto	35.9
stave	35.9
upriver	35.9
wicket	35.9
searchlight	35.8
vagabond	35.8
coachman	35.7
empress	35.7
hack	35.7
highroad	35.7
pinnacle	35.7
prone	35.7
tally	35.7
anemone	35.6
bazaar	35.6
crossroad	35.6
distract	35.6
flurry	35.6
glint	35.6
shrew	35.6
thereabouts	35.6
cinema	35.5
ego	35.5
simmer	35.5
bobcat	35.4
graft	35.4
shuttle	35.4
venom	35.4
wherefore	35.4
boron	35.3
cosmos	35.3
lard	35.3
outback	35.3
phylum	35.3
vertebrae	35.3
vomit	35.3
lawless	35.2
pedigree	35.2
pew	35.2
reportedly	35.2
solder	35.2
ember	35.1
sawhorse	35.1
coppersmith	35.0
dissect	35.0
inferno	35.0
slither	35.0
bin	34.9
durability	34.9
lawbreaker	34.9
noteworthy	34.9
novice	34.9
rut	34.9
sanity	34.9
tarnish	34.9
trellis	34.9
deceive	34.8
disarray	34.8
eyesore	34.8
icebreaker	34.8
initiate	34.8
invaluable	34.8
rupture	34.8
scallop	34.8
sluice	34.8
swerve	34.8
adept	34.7
airborne	34.7
barb	34.7
cramp	34.7
froth	34.7
hemoglobin	34.7
lukewarm	34.7
moor	34.7
muck	34.7
swivel	34.7
valor	34.7
dredge	34.6
flinch	34.6
glockenspiel	34.6
scepter	34.6
trigonometry	34.6
yearn	34.6
affix	34.4
excavate	34.4
entrust	34.3
tendon	34.3
anthracite	34.2
breakwater	34.2
succulent	34.2
deflect	34.1
ensemble	34.1
animate	34.0
bluntly	34.0
cartload	34.0
clerical	34.0
coma	34.0
dub	34.0
furnishing	34.0
furthermore	34.0
gash	34.0
geographer	34.0
hearsay	34.0
heartsick	34.0
infringe	34.0
jawbone	34.0
mystify	34.0
rehabilitate	34.0
rover	34.0
saddlebag	34.0
skewer	34.0
stevedore	34.0
stupor	34.0
thunderstruck	34.0
ace	33.9
bestow	33.9
bridegroom	33.9
clod	33.9
corporal	33.9
corrode	33.9
crinkle	33.9
endanger	33.9
lurk	33.9
madame	33.9
marksman	33.9
mimeograph	33.9
ponder	33.9
portrayal	33.9
recollect	33.9
savor	33.9
sickle	33.9
spry	33.9
threescore	33.9
timberland	33.9
tombstone	33.9
windfall	33.9
curvature	33.8
krypton	33.8
muddle	33.8
outnumber	33.8
whalebone	33.8
confide	33.7
contractor	33.7
cripple	33.7
czar	33.7
dilute	33.7
kettledrum	33.7
keynote	33.7
switchboard	33.7
marathon	33.6
repent	33.6
supervisor	33.6
sympathize	33.6
crosscut	33.5
relic	33.5
seaway	33.5
abbot	33.3
barium	33.3
blacken	33.3
blemish	33.3
hustle	33.3
invasion	33.3
knead	33.3
mishap	33.3
obstinate	33.3
wonderland	33.3
caretaker	33.2
craftsman	33.2

Word	Value	Word	Value	Word	Value	Word	Value
hag	33.2	sunspot	31.3	sorcery	30.6	**Sixth Grade**	
halfback	33.2	tactful	31.3	topaz	30.6		
hostage	33.2	toddle	31.3	tuxedo	30.6	cuspid	29.0
putt	33.2	whomever	31.3	urn	30.6	erode	29.0
timekeeper	33.2	garnish	31.2	wrongdoer	30.6	ventricle	29.0
pare	33.1	cipher	31.1	abstain	30.5	broker	28.9
extinguisher	33.0	genesis	31.1	adore	30.5	causeway	28.9
spawn	33.0	inkwell	31.1	afflict	30.5	tread	28.8
conceit	32.9	jackal	31.1	amethyst	30.5	byway	28.7
stagnant	32.9	preen	31.1	analogy	30.5	topcoat	28.7
ream	32.7	retort	31.1	arson	30.5	linseed	28.6
wafer	32.7	calligraphy	31.0	backwater	30.5	rigor	28.6
beryllium	32.6	diligent	31.0	bunker	30.5	synagogue	28.6
lubricate	32.6	dour	31.0	carload	30.5	underhanded	28.6
molar	32.6	yule	31.0	defer	30.5	blackhead	28.5
protectorate	32.6	serenade	30.9	ditty	30.5	ironwork	28.4
septic	32.6	decor	30.8	enigma	30.5	stucco	28.4
spearhead	32.6	gladiator	30.8	fireproof	30.5	typhoon	28.4
stellar	32.6	redeem	30.8	fortification	30.5	doldrums	27.7
detach	32.5	Reno	30.8	gusher	30.5	sterilize	27.7
disrupt	32.5	respire	30.8	infect	30.5	cabinetmaker	27.6
transfusion	32.3	beriberi	30.7	jounce	30.5	wardroom	27.3
unjustly	32.3	bonbon	30.7	landholder	30.5	rodent	27.2
vendor	32.3	craze	30.7	ligament	30.5	corp	26.9
draftsman	32.2	drudge	30.7	memo	30.5	parabola	26.5
err	32.2	forthcoming	30.7	nevermore	30.5	chivalry	26.4
hothead	32.2	goblet	30.7	ovation	30.5	versus	26.4
limerick	32.2	gusto	30.7	ringside	30.5	chronology	26.2
reside	32.2	initiation	30.7	schoolfellow	30.5	quintet	26.1
slur	32.2	isolate	30.7	shackle	30.5	soloist	26.1
calamity	32.1	lifesaver	30.7	sharecropper	30.5	cowlick	26.0
caress	32.1	mantis	30.7	shipshape	30.5	headgear	26.0
comeback	32.1	nape	30.7	smolder	30.5	afterlife	25.9
deteriorate	32.1	narcotic	30.7	swath	30.5	fanatic	25.9
gauntlet	32.1	overrun	30.7	twinge	30.5	hothouse	25.9
rummage	32.1	scald	30.7	warble	30.5	fishery	25.0
sideboard	32.1	shoddy	30.7	apostle	30.4	spinet	24.6
superficially	32.1	snag	30.7	balk	30.4	squabble	24.6
technician	32.1	ambiguous	30.6	baste	30.4	talon	24.6
enzyme	32.0	amuck	30.6	fjord	30.4	veneer	24.6
flagship	32.0	billboard	30.6	ghoul	30.4	wisecrack	24.6
hairline	32.0	brawn	30.6	hovel	30.4	backfield	23.9
hearthstone	32.0	comely	30.6	peddle	30.4	clapboard	23.9
townsman	32.0	congest	30.6	retrieve	30.4	convent	23.9
doeskin	31.9	contingent	30.6	sinuous	30.4	natal	23.9
homer	31.9	cornstarch	30.6	straddle	30.4	obverse	23.9
knapsack	31.9	dignitary	30.6	brigade	30.2	steeplechase	23.9
onlooker	31.9	discoverer	30.6	dinghy	30.2	toggle	23.9
deduct	31.7	dunk	30.6	lingerie	30.2	valise	23.9
gneiss	31.7	fiancé	30.6	molest	30.2	confound	23.7
descendant	31.6	fillet	30.6	scour	30.2	detain	23.7
hale	31.6	gunwale	30.6	disloyalty	30.1	furl	23.7
impair	31.6	hangman	30.6	watercress	30.1	jamb	23.7
wildfire	31.6	hookup	30.6	backhand	29.6	sandbank	23.7
archeologist	31.5	immaculate	30.6	bung	29.6	shortcake	23.7
oxidize	31.5	jeer	30.6	caption	29.6	appall	23.2
sequin	31.5	mania	30.6	chasm	29.6	incubate	23.2
midstream	31.4	moron	30.6	crosspiece	29.6	osmosis	23.2
radioactive	31.4	nutmeg	30.6	letup	29.6	mandolin	22.1
rivet	31.4	pendant	30.6	pamper	29.6	sane	22.1
derby	31.3	rant	30.6	tress	29.6	bumble	16.5
etch	31.3	rape	30.6	chromatic	29.5		
intern	31.3	rave	30.6	bridesmaid	29.4		
pemmican	31.3	signboard	30.6	petite	29.2		

surly	56.0	foremost	44.7	brandy	42.5	imperative	40.7
spite	54.8	heed	44.7	illusion	42.5	outright	40.7
extend	53.4	revere	44.7	indignation	42.4	provisions	40.7
sward	51.9	exceedingly	44.6	mower	42.4	advocate	40.6
extent	51.7	naturalist	44.6	versatile	42.4	periodic	40.6
commission	50.4	perspective	44.5	cerebrum	42.3	straightedge	40.6
physics	50.4	microscopic	44.4	dynasty	42.3	austere	40.5
remote	50.1	distribute	44.2	brine	42.2	nightingale	40.5
welfare	50.0	genus	44.2	comrade	42.2	pitchblende	40.5
precisely	49.9	venison	44.2	varsity	42.2	terrace	40.5
era	49.7	controversy	44.1	masterpiece	42.1	ungainly	40.5
architecture	49.3	rum	44.1	originate	42.1	explicit	40.4
secondary	49.3	component	44.0	sparse	42.1	futile	40.4
interpretation	49.0	din	44.0	generic	42.0	pension	40.4
aspect	48.5	nautical	44.0	psychology	42.0	revenue	40.4
catholic	48.4	tract	44.0	sequoia	42.0	solvent	40.4
statistics	48.4	exclusively	43.9	annex	41.9	stark	40.4
virtually	48.3	historian	43.9	endeavor	41.9	testify	40.4
warren	48.2	keel	43.9	pomp	41.9	imperial	40.3
dominate	48.1	reluctant	43.9	diverse	41.8	navigable	40.3
convert	47.7	faculty	43.8	malice	41.8	astute	40.2
specimen	47.6	quest	43.8	whey	41.8	chronic	40.2
relate	47.5	exceptionally	43.7	abound	41.7	cite	40.2
encounter	47.2	playwright	43.7	blueprint	41.7	closure	40.2
phase	47.2	portable	43.7	critic	41.7	consul	40.2
sufficiently	46.9	specialist	43.7	pike	41.7	knell	40.2
hull	46.8	visualize	43.7	quota	41.7	pallet	40.2
infinite	46.8	ward	43.7	inequality	41.6	passive	40.2
caddie	46.6	feudal	43.6	seafaring	41.6	pungent	40.2
extension	46.6	patriot	43.5	epic	41.4	anguish	40.1
gesture	46.6	virtue	43.5	mahogany	41.4	poise	40.1
cardinal	46.5	exert	43.4	revive	41.4	proclaim	40.1
dictator	46.5	resign	43.4	crusade	41.3	violate	40.1
rayon	46.4	sloth	43.4	exploit	41.3	adverse	40.0
transmitter	46.4	perpetual	43.3	galleon	41.3	epoch	40.0
tavern	46.1	specifically	43.3	jot	41.3	repose	40.0
emerge	46.0	defendant	43.2	via	41.3	discern	39.9
fez	46.0	maneuver	43.2	clergyman	41.2	frivolous	39.9
preliminary	46.0	anatomy	43.1	haunch	41.2	scrimmage	39.9
bide	45.9	fission	43.1	imply	41.2	feud	39.8
constitute	45.9	steward	43.1	lathe	41.2	fiat	39.8
compromise	45.8	veal	43.1	maternal	41.2	masthead	39.8
melancholy	45.7	yoke	43.1	marrow	41.1	painstaking	39.8
ultimate	45.7	anvil	43.0	sustain	41.1	prudent	39.8
catfish	45.6	buckwheat	43.0	belfry	41.0	residue	39.8
correspond	45.6	dimension	43.0	lavish	41.0	scant	39.8
desolate	45.6	kin	43.0	nominal	41.0	copperhead	39.7
formidable	45.5	transmission	43.0	precede	41.0	counselor	39.7
clipper	45.4	academic	42.9	propaganda	41.0	emit	39.7
kerosene	45.4	devote	42.9	savanna	41.0	registers	39.7
pivot	45.3	meager	42.9	suet	41.0	subordinate	39.7
artillery	45.2	rendezvous	42.9	zeal	41.0	tumult	39.7
mutual	45.2	sage	42.9	dictate	40.9	vertex	39.7
resemblance	45.2	cope	42.8	induce	40.9	vocation	39.7
abacus	45.1	galley	42.8	integrity	40.9	astern	39.6
exotic	45.1	legitimate	42.8	turbulent	40.9	dilemma	39.6
realm	45.1	sentiment	42.8	veto	40.9	eminent	39.6
agony	45.0	fusion	42.7	delicacy	40.8	manifest	39.6
deliberate	45.0	inheritance	42.6	myriad	40.8	culprit	39.5
congruous	44.9	minstrel	42.6	sloop	40.8	etiquette	39.5
scope	44.9	placid	42.6	vengeance	40.8	researcher	39.5
quarry	44.8	wireless	42.6	immigrant	40.7	tentative	39.5

Word		Word		Word		Seventh and Eighth Grades	
virtual	39.5	embark	38.6	havoc	37.7		
aloof	39.4	fraud	38.6	posterity	37.7	jubilation	36.8
elite	39.4	guttural	38.6	rasp	37.7	kingfisher	36.8
engulf	39.4	lubrication	38.6	docile	37.6	lenient	36.8
niche	39.4	monotony	38.6	exempt	37.6	lightship	36.8
pious	39.4	obsolete	38.6	taper	37.6	martial	36.8
aghast	39.3	surrey	38.6	tinker	37.6	neuron	36.8
articulate	39.3	aristocracy	38.5	flit	37.5	periscope	36.8
conversely	39.3	arrogant	38.5	pastoral	37.5	sauerkraut	36.8
intercept	39.3	darn	38.5	scarcity	37.5	adolescent	36.7
prolific	39.3	foodstuff	38.5	volatile	37.5	amiable	36.7
prostrate	39.3	irony	38.5	beseech	37.4	apex	36.7
quicksilver	39.3	succotash	38.5	gallows	37.4	attrition	36.7
signify	39.3	unanimous	38.5	mingle	37.4	bulkhead	36.7
thesis	39.3	communist	38.4	telecast	37.4	concede	36.7
thoroughbred	39.3	excise	38.4	abyss	37.3	converge	36.7
compensate	39.2	greenhorn	38.4	cropland	37.3	councilor	36.7
literal	39.2	suffice	38.4	dispense	37.3	cravat	36.7
livery	39.2	cowbird	38.3	hulk	37.3	dominion	36.7
oblique	39.2	cranium	38.3	stringent	37.3	expire	36.7
reproach	39.2	finite	38.3	deter	37.2	grisly	36.7
adjoin	39.1	incumbent	38.3	saber	37.2	harry	36.7
adjourn	39.1	sorrel	38.3	stylus	37.2	inveterate	36.7
bullfinch	39.1	alluvial	38.2	chivalrous	37.1	malady	36.7
corrupt	39.1	cerebellum	38.2	crepe	37.1	ration	36.7
diffusion	39.1	commodity	38.2	heavyweight	37.1	suffrage	36.7
gape	39.1	confine	38.2	latent	37.1	tattoo	36.7
straightway	39.1	disperse	38.2	maxim	37.1	thoroughfare	36.7
superficial	39.1	extravagant	38.2	payload	37.1	disdain	36.6
cherish	39.0	fervent	38.2	seagoing	37.1	discord	36.5
contend	39.0	fireball	38.2	abode	37.0	flagon	36.5
dashboard	39.0	humiliation	38.2	benign	37.0	gaff	36.5
excursion	39.0	inasmuch	38.2	capability	37.0	gasket	36.5
folly	39.0	candid	38.1	lawsuit	37.0	precipice	36.5
guerilla	39.0	commend	38.1	mirage	37.0	sardine	36.5
lament	39.0	deposition	38.1	mire	37.0	stalwart	36.5
chassis	38.9	deprive	38.1	recoil	37.0	auger	36.4
diffuse	38.9	encompass	38.1	restrict	37.0	axiom	36.4
inauguration	38.9	equinox	38.1	swine	37.0	bland	36.4
lawmaker	38.9	optimism	38.1	acoustic	36.9	bliss	36.4
omen	38.9	parody	38.1	addict	36.9	downgrade	36.4
sarcasm	38.9	pestle	38.1	assert	36.9	indulge	36.4
sterling	38.9	presume	38.1	commune	36.9	squalid	36.4
tenor	38.9	fallacy	38.0	complacent	36.9	bunting	36.3
vile	38.9	flywheel	38.0	curry	36.9	scrutiny	36.3
zenith	38.9	baffle	37.9	downcast	36.9	transplant	36.3
benevolent	38.8	destroyer	37.9	fauna	36.9	bluster	36.2
contemplate	38.8	junta	37.9	gossamer	36.9	impartial	36.2
esteem	38.8	oblivion	37.9	homily	36.9	infernal	36.2
flux	38.8	reformatory	37.9	ironclad	36.9	photon	36.2
gouge	38.8	atoll	37.8	leeway	36.9	vernal	36.2
habitual	38.8	blithe	37.8	nationalist	36.9	wistful	36.2
paradox	38.8	cantilever	37.8	rickets	36.9	yawl	36.2
tote	38.8	dank	37.8	ambrosia	36.8	assent	36.1
boost	38.7	dexter	37.8	awl	36.8	bitch	36.1
breach	38.7	fiend	37.8	bile	36.8	bloodshot	36.1
forfeit	38.7	hominy	37.8	cavalier	36.8	cachet	36.1
isle	38.7	magistrate	37.8	confront	36.8	caviar	36.1
sandpiper	38.7	paddock	37.8	convoy	36.8	deficient	36.1
tanner	38.7	precincts	37.8	duckbill	36.8	divert	36.1
truce	38.7	resume	37.8	embassy	36.8	garret	36.1
turnpike	38.7	skiff	37.8	enlist	36.8	gavel	36.1
vantage	38.7	wisp	37.8	gondola	36.8	hedgerow	36.1
ale	38.6	breadfruit	37.7	harrow	36.8		

Seventh and Eighth Grades

Word	Score	Word	Score	Word	Score	Word	Score
innards	36.1	bituminous	35.3	mores	34.5	consecrate	33.9
nomad	36.1	brindle	35.3	semantics	34.5	dawdle	33.9
rhetoric	36.1	carnivorous	35.3	lethal	34.4	epitaph	33.9
slander	36.1	ebony	35.3	pensive	34.4	festoon	33.9
abet	36.0	guild	35.3	strident	34.4	foyer	33.9
bookkeeping	36.0	intuition	35.3	warhead	34.4	gamut	33.9
evoke	36.0	toxic	35.3	corona	34.3	genital	33.9
feudalism	36.0	zoology	35.3	virile	34.3	grapple	33.9
flail	36.0	bypass	35.2	agitate	34.2	harass	33.9
mainstay	36.0	deity	35.2	perverse	34.2	heartfelt	33.9
oblige	36.0	manipulate	35.2	tact	34.2	homage	33.9
provoke	36.0	orthodox	35.2	cutaway	34.1	impetuous	33.9
quench	36.0	ragtime	35.2	dowel	34.1	intrepid	33.9
renown	36.0	southpaw	35.2	succumb	34.1	loath	33.9
sever	36.0	corkscrew	35.1	trinity	34.1	luscious	33.9
socialist	36.0	edit	35.1	allegory	34.0	proficient	33.9
sordid	36.0	gala	35.1	allot	34.0	revel	33.9
treachery	36.0	lucid	35.1	apathy	34.0	rogue	33.9
catwalk	35.9	scalpel	35.1	assess	34.0	safari	33.9
disciple	35.9	serf	35.1	autonomy	34.0	towpath	33.9
entity	35.9	spasm	35.1	beechnut	34.0	vagrant	33.9
evade	35.9	trek	35.1	belligerent	34.0	verve	33.9
gadfly	35.9	cantankerous	35.0	benediction	34.0	woof	33.9
impudent	35.9	cram	35.0	coffer	34.0	aqualung	33.8
jovial	35.9	curt	35.0	contrive	34.0	crux	33.8
quadruple	35.9	curtsy	35.0	cordial	34.0	expel	33.8
rapier	35.9	custard	35.0	cosmopolitan	34.0	keystone	33.8
rowdy	35.9	fissure	35.0	cuisine	34.0	palate	33.8
scuff	35.9	hacksaw	35.0	detriment	34.0	piecemeal	33.8
oust	35.8	madrigal	35.0	doughty	34.0	poop	33.8
fallout	35.7	mandate	35.0	edict	34.0	viscous	33.8
interlude	35.7	relevant	35.0	envoy	34.0	womb	33.8
pact	35.7	utopia	35.0	ethnic	34.0	caliber	33.7
ravenous	35.7	waterworks	35.0	friar	34.0	jostle	33.7
sham	35.7	allegedly	34.9	genial	34.0	martyr	33.7
supple	35.7	compile	34.9	gristmill	34.0	shoal	33.7
woo	35.7	coup	34.9	javelin	34.0	siphon	33.7
baleful	35.6	enroll	34.9	millennium	34.0	suture	33.7
buttress	35.6	ethics	34.9	motorcade	34.0	sylvan	33.7
corporate	35.6	expressway	34.9	namesake	34.0	amulet	33.6
gable	35.6	lucrative	34.9	pap	34.0	dissent	33.6
gangway	35.6	opportune	34.9	perplex	34.0	eider	33.6
joss	35.6	oracle	34.9	platoon	34.0	fetus	33.6
mediocre	35.6	pavilion	34.9	profess	34.0	trowel	33.6
monologue	35.6	rue	34.9	prudence	34.0	vodka	33.6
mooring	35.6	boardinghouse	34.8	ratify	34.0	affinity	33.5
piebald	35.6	contradict	34.8	sanction	34.0	exhort	33.5
roadbed	35.6	lax	34.8	scandal	34.0	hallucination	33.5
shuck	35.6	portly	34.8	scarp	34.0	moonshine	33.5
waif	35.6	pretext	34.8	seaworthy	34.0	poultice	33.5
whatsoever	35.6	sodden	34.8	shortwave	34.0	specter	33.5
wince	35.6	thrift	34.8	spendthrift	34.0	frankfurter	33.4
adolescence	35.5	winch	34.8	treadmill	34.0	halibut	33.4
botany	35.5	greenwood	34.7	undermine	34.0	pontoon	33.4
depose	35.5	seismograph	34.7	valet	34.0	cocktail	33.3
hamlet	35.5	aria	34.6	victuals	34.0	dexterity	33.3
intrude	35.5	bower	34.6	whim	34.0	fainthearted	33.3
sabotage	35.5	mucilage	34.6	withers	34.0	farce	33.2
cadence	35.4	aggregate	34.5	bolster	33.9	frugal	33.2
detract	35.4	avid	34.5	brawl	33.9	gruesome	33.2
pretzel	35.4	batten	34.5	canter	33.9	guile	33.2
abolish	35.3	biotic	34.5	catapult	33.9	heath	33.2
		boisterous	34.5	chronicle	33.9	noxious	33.2
		maverick	34.5	colossus	33.9	replica	33.2

swarthy	33.2	halftone	32.0	cocksure	30.7
tartar	33.2	paroxysm	32.0	copyright	30.7
allspice	33.1	rapport	32.0	dell	30.7
transverse	33.1	reconnaissance	32.0	fetter	30.7
infest	33.0	shroud	32.0	filigree	30.7
interim	33.0	stealth	32.0	initially	30.7
loophole	33.0	conjure	31.9	inmate	30.7
panhandle	33.0	discourse	31.9	limousine	30.7
sludge	33.0	discriminate	31.9	obliterate	30.7
stow	33.0	gargoyle	31.9	openwork	30.7
traction	33.0	indenture	31.9	parley	30.7
nostalgia	32.9	jaunty	31.9	rusk	30.7
taint	32.9	overuse	31.9	spree	30.7
fatherland	32.8	renegade	31.9	ultra	30.7
silverfish	32.8	taunt	31.9	upstart	30.7
traverse	32.8	anoint	31.8	visa	30.7
intervene	32.7	blatant	31.8	abusive	30.6
pert	32.7	forum	31.8	adamant	30.6
assassin	32.6	albeit	31.7	amend	30.6
brusque	32.6	birthrate	31.7	anthology	30.6
centennial	32.6	dispel	31.7	bloodthirsty	30.6
distill	32.6	lethargy	31.7	capitulate	30.6
doomsday	32.6	scow	31.7	careworn	30.6
excrete	32.6	stonework	31.7	carpetbag	30.6
hookworm	32.6	burlesque	31.6	certify	30.6
lorry	32.6	concise	31.6	cleave	30.6
oligarchy	32.6	lampblack	31.6	cog	30.6
tenuous	32.6	psyche	31.6	coif	30.6
travois	32.6	smite	31.6	condone	30.6
tribulation	32.6	cadaver	31.5	confection	30.6
wattle	32.6	cicada	31.5	consolidate	30.6
inter	32.5	fraternal	31.5	dirge	30.6
nova	32.5	miser	31.5	euphemism	30.6
literate	32.4	posterior	31.5	feline	30.6
tweed	32.4	titanic	31.5	forthright	30.6
daft	32.3	bogus	31.4	frock	30.6
galore	32.3	bushman	31.4	garish	30.6
lust	32.3	earmark	31.4	grotto	30.6
nonchalant	32.3	kindle	31.4	gunny	30.6
revulsion	32.3	adroit	31.3	hazelnut	30.6
taboo	32.3	affluent	31.3	hearse	30.6
archive	32.2	bumpkin	31.3	ingot	30.6
loin	32.2	comply	31.3	invoke	30.6
matron	32.2	contemplation	31.3	jowl	30.6
prelude	32.2	entitle	31.3	meddle	30.6
triad	32.2	eyestrain	31.3	muse	30.6
unscrupulous	32.2	freeman	31.3	obituary	30.6
aster	32.1	levee	31.3	palisade	30.6
breech	32.1	lifeline	31.3	primal	30.6
domicile	32.1	canine	31.1	promontory	30.6
enunciate	32.1	gazette	31.1	rebuff	30.6
gearbox	32.1	recount	31.1	recalcitrant	30.6
impunity	32.1	amalgam	31.0	recuperate	30.6
ledger	32.1	derelict	31.0	rite	30.6
limpid	32.1	grog	31.0	scavenge	30.6
pertain	32.1	horsetail	31.0	sidelong	30.6
prestigious	32.1	lifeblood	31.0	skeptic	30.6
sty	32.1	satchel	31.0	snuffbox	30.6
veld	32.1	tidbit	31.0	sweetmeats	30.6
waft	32.1	borough	30.8	tankard	30.6
dogma	32.0	chaff	30.8	taw	30.6
electroscope	32.0	teletype	30.8	vassal	30.6
fidelity	32.0	viaduct	30.8	verdant	30.6
gird	32.0	beryl	30.7	vouch	30.6

Seventh and Eighth Grades

whit	30.6
wildfowl	30.6
acquit	30.5
alms	30.5
anaconda	30.5
archeology	30.5
bicker	30.5
bloat	30.5
brushwood	30.5
cohort	30.5
commute	30.5
conduit	30.5
deduce	30.5
deem	30.5
delectable	30.5
depreciate	30.5
destitute	30.5
encore	30.5
enliven	30.5
expend	30.5
extant	30.5
farseeing	30.5
fascinate	30.5
fiasco	30.5
gentlefolk	30.5
gizzard	30.5
gooseberry	30.5
greenback	30.5
hairbreadth	30.5
harem	30.5
heinous	30.5
humdrum	30.5
hysteria	30.5
impede	30.5
instill	30.5
jargon	30.5
knave	30.5
lineman	30.5
ludicrous	30.5
lurid	30.5
mackintosh	30.5
magnanimous	30.5
maroon	30.5
marquis	30.5
mart	30.5
maul	30.5
mayfly	30.5
oarlock	30.5
obese	30.5
palsy	30.5
paltry	30.5
paragon	30.5
preposterous	30.5
privy	30.5
prosecutor	30.5
purport	30.5
putrid	30.5
saga	30.5
scotch	30.5
scruple	30.5
snipe	30.5
stratum	30.5

Word	Value		Word	Value		Word	Value		Word	Value
subside	30.5		captious	29.6		sedge	26.2		quay	23.7
surmise	30.5		cock-eyed	29.6		meander	26.0		dismantle	23.4
sweepstakes	30.5		elderberry	29.6		veer	26.0		epistle	23.4
swindle	30.5		fanatical	29.6		gist	25.9		recline	23.4
swordplay	30.5		hatchway	29.6		ordain	25.9		chatterbox	23.3
tabby	30.5		loiter	29.6		pleat	25.9		chide	23.3
tenacity	30.5		peppercorn	29.6		superintend	25.9		doff	23.3
tomfoolery	30.5		smock	29.6		teakwood	25.9		dram	23.3
truss	30.5		transfix	29.6		agnostic	25.6		elegy	23.3
tuition	30.5		bouillon	29.3		cloister	25.6		gambol	23.3
turgid	30.5		pique	29.3		twaddle	25.6		mackinaw	23.3
vacate	30.5		vivacity	29.3		vellum	25.6		notary	23.3
vermin	30.5		halyard	29.1		matchlock	25.5		popinjay	23.3
watercourse	30.5		prom	29.1		cameo	25.2		redoubt	23.3
whet	30.5		barnacle	29.0		nonessential	25.2		reprieve	23.3
conceive	30.4		rancid	29.0		clout	25.1		sourdough	23.3
consign	30.4		roundworm	29.0		dote	25.1		syndicate	23.3
delude	30.4		aspire	28.9		extol	25.1		torchbearer	23.3
dickens	30.4		flirt	28.9		tenderfoot	25.1		allay	23.2
dirigible	30.4		gloat	28.9		bondholder	25.0		brunt	23.2
fleck	30.4		impost	28.9		commonwealth	25.0		diverge	23.2
hackle	30.4		prescribe	28.8		homogeneous	25.0		lungfish	23.2
juror	30.4		resilient	28.8		postulate	25.0		mead	23.2
lawgiver	30.4		sonnet	28.8		primate	25.0		mote	23.2
ode	30.4		fabricate	28.7		conjugate	24.8		orifice	23.2
synopsis	30.4		distraught	28.6		furlong	24.8		peon	23.2
topsail	30.4		fastidious	28.6		gantry	24.8		propagate	23.2
vanquish	30.4		jousting	28.6		cauldron	24.6		swallowtail	23.2
aviary	30.3		buffoon	28.5		flintlock	24.6		utilitarian	23.2
boldface	30.3		capsize	28.5		gunboat	24.6		aberration	23.0
caricature	30.3		labyrinth	28.4		lea	24.6		chiffon	22.1
highbrow	30.3		aura	28.1		singsong	24.6		fanfare	22.1
impel	30.3		keelboat	28.1		transact	24.6		merrymaker	22.1
tango	30.3		cutthroat	27.8		apprehend	23.9		nuance	22.1
tepid	30.3		decimeter	27.8		bittersweet	23.9		omnibus	22.1
turntable	30.3		longhorn	27.8		bugaboo	23.9		prophecy	22.1
twitter	30.3		torque	27.8		canny	23.9		rhapsody	22.1
bobtail	30.2		grange	27.7		fiscal	23.9		umbra	22.1
borderland	30.2		lactic	27.7		flange	23.9		crouton	21.1
chortle	30.2		optic	27.7		mausoleum	23.9		horseradish	21.1
guise	30.2		tapeworm	27.7		mundane	23.9		tantrum	21.1
infirm	30.2		transit	27.7		seminar	23.9		broadcloth	19.8
ire	30.2		entreat	27.3		sop	23.9		twill	19.8
journeyman	30.2		anthropology	27.2		spillway	23.9		gristle	18.1
tamp	30.2		matrix	27.2		sprocket	23.9		ravel	18.1
gusset	30.0		scone	27.2		sundry	23.9		sleazy	18.1
auricle	29.9		ulcer	27.2		tacit	23.9		woodcut	17.4
canapé	29.6		menial	26.4		chaperone	23.8		crossway	16.5
			regatta	26.4		choreography	23.8		curbstone	16.5

Words From Reading	Words From Writing	Words From Content Areas	Words From Other Sources

Name _____

Teacher _____ Year _____

	Sept.	Oct.	Nov.	Dec.	Jan.	Feb.	Mar.	Apr.	May	June	July	Aug.
100												
95												
90												
85												
80												
75												
70												
65												
60												
55												
50												
45												
40												
35												
30												
25												
20												
15												
10												
5												
0												

X—X Spelling scores
O—O Show You Know scores

Blackline #2

Literacy Plus

May be duplicated for classroom use. Zaner-Bloser, Inc.

How to Order Other Books in the Literacy Plus Series

Literacy Plus offers teachers a variety of interesting ways to use real literature in their classrooms and integrate instruction in the language arts.

The Literacy Plus Teacher Guide outlines over 180 innovative reading, writing, vocabulary, and reasoning workshops that teachers can choose from as they create their lesson plans. Workshop topics and methods are drawn from the work of leading authorities on language arts and critical thinking. Getting Started, the new introduction to the Literacy Plus program, is now included free with the Teacher Guide.

Literacy Plus Student Word Books combine the best features of a journal, dictionary, and thesaurus and use a unique semantic cluster approach to make learning new words an exciting and personal journey for students. Word Books are available in four levels for grades K-8.

New Literacy Plus Spelling puts spelling and word meaning together, where they belong. Components include a Teacher Guide to Spelling and Word Meaning *plus* My Spelling and Word Meaning Books I through III, which are designed for students to use with the program's Word Books.

To order other Literacy Plus Spelling books or purchase other Literacy Plus program materials, fill out the form below.

Type of Material	Order #	Price Each	Quantity	Total
Literacy Plus Spelling Materials				
Teacher Guide to Spelling and Word Meaning	310522	$ 29.97		$
Student Spelling Set (Grades K-2)*	310312	8.75		
Student Spelling Set (Grades 2-4)*	310314	8.75		
Student Spelling Set (Grades 4-6)*	310316	8.75		
Student Spelling Set (Grades 6-8)*	310318	8.75		
My Spelling and Word Meaning Book I (Grades 1-2)**	310531	1.98		
My Spelling and Word Meaning Book II (Grades 2-4)**	310532	1.98		
My Spelling and Word Meaning Book III (Grades 4 & Up)**	310533	1.98		
Vocabulary and Spelling Game Book	310523	9.95		
Literacy Plus Program Materials				
Literacy Plus Teacher Guide	310460	$ 49.90		$
Word Book I (Grades K-2)	310401	6.95		
Word Book II (Grades 2-4)	310402	6.95		
Word Book III (Grades 4-6)	310403	6.95		
Word Book IV (Grades 6-8)	310404	6.95		

* Includes one My Spelling and Word Meaning Book *and* one accompanying Word Book.
** You should also order the accompanying Word Book.
Prices subject to change without notice.

Subtotal $_____

Tax, if applicable _____

Shipping and handling (If enclosing payment, add 8%) _____

Thank you for your order!

Total $_____

Shipping/Billing

Name _____ Position _____

School _____

School Street Address _____

City _____ State _____ ZIP _____

School Telephone (_____)

Payment ❏ Purchase Order # _____ ❏ Check # _____

❏ VISA   ❏ MasterCard   ❏ DISCOVER   Card # _____

Signature _____ Expiration Date _____

Mail To
Zaner-Bloser
Educational Publishers
2200 W. 5th Ave.
P.O. Box 16764
Columbus, OH 43216-6764

Toll-Free Ordering
1-800-421-3018

Zaner-Bloser
Brings Learning to Life

3070